S. Hrg. 113–277

PARTNERSHIPS TO ADVANCE THE BUSINESS OF SPACE

HEARING

BEFORE THE

SUBCOMMITTEE ON SCIENCE AND SPACE

OF THE

COMMITTEE ON COMMERCE, SCIENCE, AND TRANSPORTATION UNITED STATES SENATE

ONE HUNDRED THIRTEENTH CONGRESS

FIRST SESSION

———

MAY 16, 2013

———

Printed for the use of the Committee on Commerce, Science, and Transportation

U.S. GOVERNMENT PRINTING OFFICE

87–972 PDF   WASHINGTON : 2014

For sale by the Superintendent of Documents, U.S. Government Printing Office
Internet: bookstore.gpo.gov   Phone: toll free (866) 512–1800; DC area (202) 512–1800
Fax: (202) 512–2104   Mail: Stop IDCC, Washington, DC 20402–0001

CONTENTS

                                                                                        Page
Hearing held on May 16, 2013 1
Statement of Senator Nelson 1
    Prepared statement 3
Statement of Senator Coats 1
Statement of Senator Cruz 2

WITNESSES

N. Wayne Hale, Jr., Director of Human Spaceflight, Special Aerospace Ser-
    vices, NASA Flight Director and Program Manager (Ret.) 4
    Prepared statement 6
Patti Grace Smith, Principal, Patti Grace Smith Consulting, LLC 8
    Prepared statement 10
Captain Michael Lopez-Alegria, USN (Ret.), President, Commercial
    Spaceflight Federation 14
    Prepared statement 15
Dr. Steven H. Collicott, Professor, Purdue University School of Aeronautics
    and Astronautics 22
    Prepared statement 24

APPENDIX

Response to written questions submitted by Hon. Bill Nelson to:
    N. Wayne Hale, Jr. 39
    Patti Grace Smith 41
    Captain Michael Lopez-Alegria 42
    Dr. Steven H. Collicott 44

PARTNERSHIPS TO ADVANCE
THE BUSINESS OF SPACE

THURSDAY, MAY 16, 2013

U.S. SENATE,
SUBCOMMITTEE ON SCIENCE AND SPACE,
COMMITTEE ON COMMERCE, SCIENCE, AND TRANSPORTATION,
Washington, DC.

The Subcommittee met, pursuant to notice, at 10:06 a.m. in room 253, Russell Senate Office Building, Hon. Bill Nelson, Chairman of the Subcommittee, presiding.

OPENING STATEMENT OF HON. BILL NELSON,
U.S. SENATOR FROM FLORIDA

Senator NELSON. Good morning. As an accommodation to the Senator from Indiana, who wants to make a special introduction, Senator Cruz and I will turn to him first.

STATEMENT OF HON. DAN COATS,
U.S. SENATOR FROM INDIANA

Senator COATS. Mr. Chairman and Senator Cruz, I thank you for the privilege of doing this. I commend both you and Senator Cruz for your leadership on this.

It's a real pleasure for me to introduce a distinguished constituent from Purdue University, Steven Collicott. Dr. Steven Collicott is an expert in his field. He received his undergraduate degree from the University of Michigan and his Master's from Stanford, but joined the Purdue faculty in West Lafayette, Indiana in 1991, where he is a Professor in the School of Aeronautics and Astronautics.

As you know, Mr. Chairman, our Aero-Astro program at Purdue is fairly well-known. Twenty-two astronauts have come out of Purdue and flown, maybe one of them with you on your flight. I'm not so sure about that.

Senator NELSON. Do you know the institution that has produced more than any other university?

Senator COATS. I'd love to say it was Purdue, but I think you are probably going to name some university in Florida.

Senator NELSON. No. It is actually the Naval Academy.

Senator COATS. Oh, really? OK. That makes sense. The ultimate in flying assignments.

But such notables as Gus Grissom and Neil Armstrong and many, many others have come out of the Purdue program. Dr. Collicott has led a team of students in providing an experimental project that will be operated on the International Space Station and a number of other distinguished accomplishments. So I want to just welcome him here today.

I would love to stay, but other Subcommittees have made other callings, so I have to excuse myself on that. But I thank you for the opportunity to introduce Dr. Collicott.

Senator NELSON. Thank you so much.

Senator Cruz?

STATEMENT OF HON. TED CRUZ, U.S. SENATOR FROM TEXAS

Senator CRUZ. Well, thank you, Mr. Chairman. Thank you to each of the witnesses who are here today. I thank you, Mr. Chairman, for the opportunity for us to have this hearing and to get to know more about the exciting potential for advancing our space-related knowledge and achievement by taking advantage of the competitive forces and creative drive of the private sector.

Our economy has a great stake in the space race. Last year, 78 orbital launches were conducted worldwide, 20 of which were commercial launches. And those 20 launches generated more than $2.4 billion in revenues, of which an estimated $108 million was attributed to U.S. launches. Activity in the space industry creates good, high-tech jobs now, and it inspires our next generation of leaders as well.

For years, the U.S. Government has worked as a partner with the commercial space industry, and the NASA Authorization Act of 2010 set in place a productive balance between the two that continues to bear fruit.

Today, I look forward to hearing from our panel about how we can achieve even greater efficiencies from that balance and how we can encourage more significant investment from the commercial space industry and what legal and regulatory challenges are presented by its future development.

Thank you, Mr. Chairman.

Senator NELSON. Thank you.

As you can see, we run things a little differently on this committee. We are a little more informal. But when it gets to the subject of commercial space, it becomes extremely important. It becomes extremely important that we get American vehicles flying Americans back up to the Space Station. It's extremely important that we have vehicles that are designed to be as safe as possible, as the new generation of rockets are being designed. It was certainly an admonition of the Gehman Commission that investigated the last Space Shuttle disaster that said that once you have completed the Space Station with the Space Shuttle, you shut it down and you replace it with a safer rocket. Of course, that is being designed right now.

We see the new applications of commercial activity in space, and although we have always had—basically, it has been the contractors that have produced the hardware and the systems under NASA's direction that has given us this extraordinarily successful program. It now enters a new dimension of commercial space.

I just came from a meeting with the President's nominee for the Department of Transportation, and we discussed how it is very important that the Office of Commercial Space Transportation in the

Department of Transportation understands that they should never get into these stovepipes that are so typical in government, where turf becomes more important than the mission, and then the turf battles and all the little jealousies occur.

And the Department of Transportation, I shared with the nominee, should do what their mission is, which is to handle administratively and let NASA do what NASA does best and not try to compete with each other.

Now, we are going to be doing a NASA authorization bill this year, and we also plan to update the Commercial Space Launch Act. So we are going to be using these hearings to help us develop the policy that will continue to guide our space community toward the goal of exploring the heavens.

So there is a lot to discuss, suborbital space, and I am going to insert in the record my comments.

[The prepared statement of Senator Nelson follows:]

PREPARED STATEMENT OF HON. BILL NELSON, U.S. SENATOR FROM FLORIDA

Good morning! Thank you all for being here today for the third Science and Space Subcommittee hearing of this Congress. In today's hearing, we will hear about private sector partnerships with the Federal Government on suborbital and orbital space flight and the opportunities these capabilities afford this nation in advancing the space industry.

As you may know, we will be reauthorizing NASA this year and updating the Commercial Space Launch Act (CSLA). We will be using these hearings to help develop the policy that will continue to guide the space community toward our goal of getting people to Mars. And we cannot reach this goal without the likes of the private and civil investments.

We've discussed orbital space flight in our previous hearings, but it is worth again mentioning just how promising the future is for the U.S. space industry. Since the last Authorization of NASA we have seen a lot of progress. Less than a month ago, we witnessed a successful test launch of a new rocket that will soon deliver cargo to the International Space Station, setting the stage now for two companies to conduct cargo resupply missions to the International Space Station. The second company has successfully completed two cargo delivery missions to the ISS.

NASA and its industry partners are also actively developing a commercial crew capability that will allow U.S. providers to once again send NASA astronauts to the space station. The Russians are our partners on the ISS, and we thank them for their safe delivery and return of NASA astronaut Tom Marshburn just this past Monday, among the two others, but we need our own capability as well.

Of course, NASA is also charged with building and flying the heavy-lift Space Launch System and the Orion capsule, which will take humans farther into space than ever before.

When it comes to sub-orbital space flight, I think many people are at least familiar with this market, in part because of some of the recent successes that have been publicized.

But sub-orbital space offers more than just a few minutes of weightlessness for those who can afford it. Sub-orbital space flight is also well suited to scientific research and education and can provide students and researchers with new opportunities for studying the Earth and for conducting short-duration experiments in microgravity.

We all know challenges exist, but the key to success here is balance; not just a balance between public *and* private space endeavors but also between competition *and* cooperation. As was said at our last hearing, we cannot continue to go forward with the "or" mentality. Helping to make the private space industry successful will help to send humans beyond low-Earth orbit again—and vice versa.

As we move toward updating space policy, we also need to look at the role of the Federal Aviation Administration's Office of Commercial Space Transportation in developing appropriate safety regulations for private space flight. We need to strike a balance here as well so that both government and industry can ensure safety without stifling innovation. Customer safety is a valuable component of the industry's success and if we wait too long to address this issue, an accident may compromise the whole industry.

With these issues in mind, I look forward to continuing to work with the private U.S. space industry as it is a vital part of our future space program. So, it is my pleasure to welcome all of our witnesses.

Mr. Wayne Hale, Jr. comes to us as the Director of Human Spaceflight for Special Aerospace Services. He is a retired NASA engineer who has held positions including NASA Flight Director and Space Shuttle Program Manager. Mr. Hale will discuss how commercial space efforts contribute toward national space exploration goals and the Government's role in supporting private space sector growth.

Ms. Patti Grace Smith is an Aerospace Consultant and Advisor. She has extensive experience in the U.S. space sector both as former Associate Administrator of FAA's Office of Commercial Space Transportation and as the current Chair of the NASA Advisory Council's Commercial Space Committee. Ms. Smith will address the Federal policies needs and recommendations affecting the private space industry and ways to maximize collaborations between the FAA, NASA, and private space ventures.

Captain Michael Lopez-Alegria is the President of the Commercial Spaceflight Federation. Captain Lopez-Alegria, a former NASA astronaut—and veteran of four space flights and Commander of ISS Expedition 14—now works to promote commercial spaceflight. He will provide an overview of the progress and plans of the commercial spaceflight industry as well as policy recommendations to support their efforts.

I now would like to welcome my colleague and member of this Subcommittee, Senator Coats of Indiana, to introduce our final witness from his home state.

Senator NELSON. Let me introduce our panel members.

Wayne Hale comes to us as Director of Human Spaceflight for Special Aerospace Services. He is retired from NASA. He has held positions including NASA Flight Director and Space Shuttle Program Manager. Mr. Hale is going to discuss how commercial space efforts contribute toward national space exploration goals and the government's role in supporting the private space sector growth.

Ms. Patti Grace Smith is an Aerospace Consultant and Advisor. She has extensive experience in the U.S. space sector both as a former Associate Administrator of FAA's Office of Commercial Space and as the current Chair of the NASA Advisory Council's Commercial Space Committee. She will address the Federal policies, needs, and recommendations affecting the private space industry and the ways to maximize collaborations between FAA, NASA, and private space ventures.

Captain Michael Lopez-Alegria is President of the Commercial Spaceflight Federation. A NASA astronaut, a veteran of four space flights, Commander of ISS Expedition 14, now he works to promote commercial spaceflight. He will provide an overview of the progress and plans of the commercial spaceflight industry, as well as policy recommendations.

Dr. Collicott we have already had introduced by the Senator from Indiana.

So thank you for being here and bringing your expertise to the discussion.

So, with that, Mr. Hale, we're going to put your written testimony in the record. If you will summarize it within about 5 minutes, and we will just go down the line. Thank you so much.

STATEMENT OF N. WAYNE HALE, JR., DIRECTOR OF HUMAN SPACEFLIGHT, SPECIAL AEROSPACE SERVICES, NASA FLIGHT DIRECTOR AND PROGRAM MANAGER (RET.)

Mr. HALE. Thank you, Chairman, Senator Nelson. And thank you, Ranking Member, Senator Cruz, and the entire committee, for inviting me to testify on this important matter.

In the interest of full disclosure, you should note that I spent most of my professional life working at NASA in the Space Shuttle Program. As a matter of fact, Senator Nelson, I was in Mission Control during your flight just a few years ago. During those many years, I have seen NASA at its very best and at its worst. The hard-working dedication of NASA personnel is phenomenal, and their talent and creativity are second to none. However, their endeavors have frequently been stymied due to the inherent bureaucratic inefficiencies of government work and the frequent shifts in priorities and funding that whipsaw space initiatives.

My last NASA assignment was to define the management philosophy for the new Commercial Crew Program. After leaving NASA, my work has continued as a consultant. My company, Special Aerospace Services, advises entities involved in the commercial crew and commercial space cargo enterprises, and I have volunteered my time to work with the Commercial Spaceflight Federation to establish industry standards for this fledgling community. So the Committee can see that I am hardly a disinterested party.

In space today, the most singularly vexing problem is the high cost of getting to low-Earth orbit. As Robert Heinlein once observed, "When you are in Earth orbit, you are halfway to anywhere in the universe," which accurately reflects the physics of the situation. Today, getting that first step to the universe is very costly.

Hundreds of potential business opportunities and the limitless resources of the solar system have floundered on the high cost of transportation to low-Earth orbit. Asteroid mining, energy production, and zero-gravity manufacturing are all within our grasp technologically but will not be profitable businesses until reliable and reasonably affordable transportation systems are in place.

However, these new transportation systems to low-Earth orbit have very high development costs. So we are in a chicken-or-the-egg paradox. Space business needs low-cost transportation to become profitable, while potential private transportation services need established businesses to justify the cost of their construction.

This is not the first time America has been in this situation. Both the early railroads and the fledgling air transportation industries found themselves becalmed in similar straits. The Federal taxpayer stepped in to provide critical resources to help those industries develop. These Federal investments paid back myriadfold in tax revenues when the new industries caught fire.

The history of spaceflight has been marked with the goal of decreasing the cost of transportation to low earth orbit. In the last decade, the United States has embarked on a bold new experiment to turn over the creative reins of spacecraft development to nimble, flexible, creative private commercial firms. Bolstered with a modicum of taxpayer resources, these businesses have leveraged private investment to develop new, much cheaper transportation systems.

We see the first fruits of success today with the cargo-carrying craft SpaceX's Falcon and Dragon and Orbital Science's Antares and Cygnus. These cargo-carrying, privately developed vehicles are starting to supply our government outpost, the International Space Station. In future years, the Boeing CST–100 and Sierra Nevada

Dream Chaser, both flying on the proven ULA Atlas V rocket, will be added to the fleet to carry human beings, as well as cargo.

Poised on the cusp of these new systems, America runs the risk of being penny wise and pound foolish as we make the same mistake that doomed the Space Shuttle to much higher cost operations, starving spacecraft development programs in the name of saving a few pennies for today's budget bottom line, resulting in compromised systems that, if they fly at all, will not be cheap enough to enable business in space.

Regarding NASA's deep space exploration plans, the commercial systems will enable deep space exploration initiatives in substantial ways. First, the International Space Station is our test laboratory for the critical technologies and systems that deep space exploration will need. Commercial transportation of cargo and crews to the ISS directly support deep space systems development.

As deep space exploration proceeds, commercial crew and cargo vehicles will likely be called on to aid with assembly and fuel delivery to low earth orbit. Cost-effective commercial transportation to low earth orbit can make a vital difference in equipping the space fleet. The two efforts go hand-in-hand. Funding equity between the two programs is necessary to ensure the timely success of both.

I urge Congress to fully fund both of these vital activities. They will allow America and American industries to lead in the exploration and development of human activity in our solar system. Paraphrasing John F. Kennedy, there is no project that is so important for the long-term success of humankind, and I hope that those historians of the future will record that at this crossroads of history, a creative, enterprising, farsighted nation called America led that way.

I look forward to your questions.

[The prepared statement of Mr. Hale follows:]

PREPARED STATEMENT OF N. WAYNE HALE, JR., DIRECTOR OF HUMAN SPACEFLIGHT, SPECIAL AEROSPACE SERVICES, NASA FLIGHT DIRECTOR AND PROGRAM MANAGER (RET.)

I thank the Committee for inviting me to testify concerning the growth of the space industry including the private sector space transportation.

In the interest of full disclosure, I am hardly a disinterested party in this topic. I am and have always been a passionate believer that space exploration and the industries that may derive from it will benefit humanity in ways beyond our imagining. I have spent most of my professional life working in the large government space programs of the Space Shuttle and the International Space Station. During those years I have seen NASA at its very best and at its worst. The hard working dedication of my colleagues at NASA personnel is nothing short of phenomenal, and their talent and creativity is second to none. However, their endeavors have frequently been stymied due to the inherent bureaucratic inefficiencies of government work and the frequent shifts in priorities and funding that whipsaw most space initiatives. This has led me to believe there must be a better way to develop and operate space systems.

In my last assignment before retirement from government service, I worked with Frank Bauer, the Chief Engineer of the Exploration Systems Directorate, to define the management philosophy, protocols, and processes for the then new Commercial Crew Program within NASA. After my retirement, my work has continued as a consultant. My company, Special Aerospace Services, and I are paid advisors to a number of entities involved in the commercial crew and commercial space cargo enterprises. And I have volunteered my time to work with the Commercial Spaceflight Federation to establish safety, management, and engineering standards for all the members of this fledgling industry. So the Committee can see that I am hardly a disinterested party and should weigh my testimony as such.

Establishing good, effective safety, engineering, and management standards in a voluntary industry association is the hallmark of any reputable and mature industry. I am pleased to report that the CSF is making good progress in setting up voluntary processes which will ensure public safety and promote general success in this difficult business. Industry group standards can alleviate the need for government regulations by allowing the members of a trade association to tailor best practices specifically for their industry. Evolution of these industry standards inevitably proceeds more rapidly than the development of government regulations and can therefore take rapid advantage of best practices as they emerge.

The most singularly vexing problem with space flight is the high cost of getting to low-Earth orbit. As the noted science fiction writer Robert Heinlein once observed, "when you are in earth orbit you are half way to anywhere in the universe" which accurately reflects the physics of the situation.

The lack of low cost transportation to that point located just above the earth's atmosphere and moving at 17,500 mph forward velocity has prevented potential space entrepreneurs more than any other factor. Hundreds of potential business opportunities in the limitless resources of the solar system have floundered on the high cost of transportation to low-Earth orbit. Asteroid mining, energy production, zero gravity manufacturing are all within our grasp technologically but will not be profitable until reliable and reasonably affordable transportation systems are in place.

New systems for transportation to low-Earth orbit have enormously high development costs. Private investors, with a few exceptions, are loath to provide the capital needed to develop low-Earth orbit transportation without clear and immediate business ready to purchase tickets.

So we are in a "chicken or the egg" paradox. Space business needs low cost transportation to become profitable, while potential private transportation services need established business to justify the cost of construction. This is not the first time that America has been in this situation. Both the early railroads and fledgling air transportation industries found themselves becalmed in similar straits. In both these cases, and others, the Federal taxpayers stepped in to provide critical resources to help new industries develop. Those investments have been paid back myriad-fold in tax revenues when the new industries caught fire and provided transportation systems that were the envy of the world.

NASA and its predecessor agency the NACA provided needed aeronautical research to make air transportation as inexpensive and safe as we find it today. The Federal investment in aeronautics development has paid off handsomely in the development of a multi-billion dollar industry. Indeed, one of the largest sectors of net exports in the American economy is aerospace with billion dollar sales a common occurrence.

The history of space flight—after the first early steps to demonstrate that space flight was even possible—has been marked with the goal of decreasing the cost of transportation to low-Earth orbit. In my home I have an entire shelf of books populated by volumes of studies and proposals from a multitude of thinkers spread over decades on that subject: how to provide reliable safe space transportation on the cheap.

The space system that consumed much of my professional career, the Space Shuttle, was established to achieve just such a low cost goal. But the technologies of the 1970s, harnessed to a risk adverse government apparatus resulted in a system that was only slightly less expensive than those which went before.

In the last decade, the United States embarked on a bold new experiment to turn over the creative reins of spacecraft development to entrepreneurial, nimble, flexible, creative private commercial teams. Bolstered with a modicum of taxpayer resources, these businesses have leveraged private investment to create the critical mass to develop new, much cheaper transportation systems. We see the first fruits of success today with cargo carrying craft: the SpaceX Falcon and Dragon, and the Orbital Antares and Cygnus. These cargo carrying privately developed vehicles are starting to supply our government outpost, the International Space Station. In future years others, the Boeing CST–100 and the Sierra Nevada Dream Chaser will be added to the fleet to carry human beings as well as cargo.

Poised on the cusp of these new systems, we run the risk of being penny wise and pound foolish as we make the same mistake that doomed the Space Shuttle to much higher cost operations: starving a spacecraft development program in the name of saving a few pennies for today's budget bottom line resulting in the compromised systems that, if they fly at all, will not be cheap enough to enable business in space.

This is not to devalue the development of truly deep space exploration systems by the government. Those high risk, high cost systems payback over such are long term that they would never be funded by private investment. But, like the expenses incurred by Lewis and Clark, Captain Zebulon Pike, and a host of other government expeditions in our history, the payback from exploration will be enormous for both the country and for all of humanity. Just at a more distant point in the future than business spreadsheets normally run. The SLS and the MPCV should be developed in conjunction with the commercial low-Earth orbit transportation systems. Flying to cis-lunar space to inspect a captured asteroid is an engineering and operations test worthy of a first deep space mission. But that mission can only be a first step. More should follow.

The commercial systems will enable the deep space exploration initiative in substantial ways. First of all because the ISS is our space test laboratory for the technologies and systems that deep space exploration will need. Operation in space, aboard the ISS, is the most effective means to wring out life support, communications, propulsion, and other technologies. Commercial transportation of cargo and crews to the ISS directly support deep space systems development. As deep space exploration proceeds, commercial cargo and crew vehicles will likely be called upon to aid with assembly and fuel delivery to low-Earth orbit where we will finalize preparations to head into the vasty deep. Cost effective commercial transportation to low-Earth orbit can make a vital difference in equipping the deep space fleet.

So the two efforts go hand in hand. Funding equity between the two programs is necessary to ensure the timely success of both. Currently, the commercial space effort stands uncomfortably close to the brink of financial starvation. Deep space transportation development is being stretched out by similar restrictions. Business is looking to see if the government is serious about providing the critical support or whether this effort will be wasted as so many earlier government programs which withered away on the very cusp of success: National Launch System, Orbital Space Plane, and others.

I urge the Congress to fully fund these vital activities, both the commercial crew program and the exploration systems. They will allow America and American industry to lead in the exploration and development of human activity in our solar system. When the historians of the future look back on our era, they will recognize the movement of humanity from planet earth into the solar system as the pivotal event of our times. There is no project that is so important for the long term success of humankind. I would hope that those historians record that at this crossroad of history that a creative, enterprising, farsighted nation called America led the way.

The prizes both economic and historic are too great to bypass. If America does not lead in these enterprises, somebody else will. And the leader will reap the greatest rewards both in the near term and in the longer term.

For all our limitations, America is a very rich country. There are many things which America needs to do for the present moment: provide for a strong military to protect us in a dangerous world, educate our children, care for our elderly and infirm, revitalize our transportation infrastructure of roads, bridges, airports, and more. All of these activities are of vital importance today. Space exploration is about the future. Space exploration is possibly the only line item in the Federal budget that is all about the future. Currently we spend one half of one percent of our Nation's treasure on the future. Isn't the future worth that investment?

Senator NELSON. Thank you, Mr. Hale.
Ms. Smith?

STATEMENT OF PATTI GRACE SMITH, PRINCIPAL, PATTI GRACE SMITH CONSULTING, LLC

Ms. SMITH. Mr. Chairman, Senator Cruz, and members of the Subcommittee, thank you for inviting me to be a part of this hearing. As a former Associate Administrator for Commercial Space Transportation, and as a current participant in the commercial space industry, I appreciate very much the opportunity to comment on partnerships to advance the business of space.

These are milestone times for commercial space transportation. They are times that call for a balanced approach, a balanced approach, to make sure we know how we got here, where we are, where we are going, and how to best integrate the strengths, accomplishments, and lessons of the pioneers of American spaceflight and the pioneers of new space.

Longstanding promises of commercial spaceflight are turning into visible results. SpaceX is servicing the International Space Station. Boeing recently performed a successful test of an integrated test article. Orbital Sciences has orbited a payload. Virgin Galactic has test-dropped its space passenger vehicle, all remarkable achievements that some did not expect. Sierra Nevada recently successfully completed the integrated system safety analysis review. And the list of new developers goes on and on. XCOR, Masten, Blue Origin and Armadillo Aerospace, each determined, each hopeful and relentless, each focused on safety, and all making steady progress. The Atlas rocket continues to deliver mission excellence and reliability with unparalleled success.

For years, the commercial space industry contended with skepticism. Now it must deal with the effects of enthusiasm. Both can be equally daunting. There is a risk that new enthusiasts with the best of intentions will try to change industry aims just as commercial space reaches its target. I hope that will not happen.

That is why this is a time for special discernment. When Congress approved the Commercial Space Act of 1984, one of the elements was the Office of Commercial Space Transportation, or AST, that in 1996 found a home at the FAA. That decision made it possible for early commercial space leadership to observe and absorb lessons that helped AST guide an industry from the nursery to emerging maturity.

In the 1984 Act, Congress passed legislation that created a flexible, open venue that invited opportunity rather than proscribing innovation, while permitting no compromise on safety. Over the years, entrepreneurs and regulators have worked hard to keep finding better, safer ways to conduct space flight. Congress established what became a model for space efforts in countries worldwide. The co-existence of both air and space in the FAA has forced any and all issues of how things might work out on the table.

My observation is that since before the relocation of space in the FAA, as it was formerly located in the Office of the Secretary, aviation never had to really consider it or any other new entity in its airspace. AST's presence has forced the conversation and a greater awareness of that thing we call the NAS, the National Airspace System, which is a national asset belonging to the nation, and we share it as we do all other things national.

Therefore, for the near term, I strongly favor keeping the Office of Commercial Space Transportation within the FAA as more launch manifests develop. Once that happens and space launch and space activities become a regular occurrence, a regular user in the NAS, Congress should move with deliberate speed to move AST to the Department of Transportation to take its rightful, its logical place as another transportation mode, as all other modes of transportation.

I firmly believe that this is what former Secretary Elizabeth Dole had in mind when she proposed to President Reagan that commercial space reside in the Department of Transportation during its infancy, and what former FAA Administrator David Henson had in mind when he announced to all of the FAA management team the day commercial space arrived at the FAA, and I quote, "It will be a line of business, different but equal, to all other lines of business.

We, the FAA, will enable this industry to develop to a level of robustness and routine to fulfill the dream of space as transportation." That is still the dream, and we are closer to fulfilling it than ever before.

I believe AST should continue to supervise and solely regulate suborbital commercial launch operations, including those associated with rocket launches of either humans or cargo. The FAA's Office of Commercial Space Transportation licenses the launch system as a whole, but the FAA's Office of Aviation Safety certifies the carrier aircraft when it is flying alone, even when the aircraft is operating in support of launch-related activities.

And my final point is that I strongly support extending indemnification as a recommendation at a minimum of 10 years.

I'll be happy to answer questions at the appropriate time. Thank you.

[The prepared statement of Ms. Smith follows:]

PREPARED STATEMENT OF PATTI GRACE SMITH, PRINCIPAL,
PATTI GRACE SMITH CONSULTING, LLC

Mr. Chairman, Senator Cruz, and members of the Subcommittee, thank you for inviting me to participate in this morning's hearing. My name is Patti Grace Smith and I am the Principal in Patti Grace Smith Consulting. As a former Associate Administrator of the Office of Commercial Space Transportation at the Federal Aviation Administration, and as a currently active participant in the commercial space industry, I welcome the opportunity to comment on the state of commercial space flight.

The Emergence of Commercial Space Flight

These are milestone times for commercial space transportation. These are times for a balanced approach that looks at where we have been and why; where we are today and why; and where we would like to go. I prefer an approach that considers all space capabilities, both early and new; that values the long—standing contributors who have consistently delivered unparalleled results for our nation; and similarly values the significant accomplishments of new entrants. Plans for SLS and commercial crew and cargo, it seems to me, reflect that sort of balanced approach. As an Alabamian, I am proud to say that commercial launch vehicles built in Decatur are a reality, with new ones built every year.

Today long-standing promises are turning into visible results. SpaceX, launching from Florida, has serviced the International Space Station. Orbital Sciences' Antares rocket has successfully orbited a payload from its launch site at Wallop's Island, Virginia. Virgin Galactic has test-dropped its space passenger vehicle over California as it moves closer to regular operations from New Mexico. And the Atlas V rocket is still the most reliable launch vehicle, delivering mission success one launch at a time.

These are remarkable achievements by the private sector. Yet some observers believe they are overdue when compared to America's earlier space performance. For example, President Kennedy in 1961 pledged to land a man on the moon and return him safely to Earth by the end of the decade. It took roughly 2,800 days for NASA by the time they did it in 1969. To accomplish the moon landing within this aggressive timeframe, NASA leveraged the contemporaneous capabilities of the private sector, working with industry to execute NASA's mission. NASA was the unquestioned leader, bringing the will, technical expertise, integration, and resources to the task.

Still, the commercial sector has delivered convincingly, as well. Today, the commercial sector is demonstrating not just technical accomplishments, but vision and the willingness to take financial risks to move our relationship with space forward. On the independent initiative of private enterprise, it was also roughly 2,800 days between October of 2004 when SpaceShipOne captured the Ansari X-Prize and May of 2012 when the SpaceX Falcon 9 docked with the International Space Station, the first for a commercial launch vehicle in the history of the Nation. Many said it couldn't be done. But SpaceX delivered, a remarkable accomplishment fully consistent with the proud tradition of American space flight.

Commercial space flight has advanced at its own measured pace during some of the darkest economic times in memory. The private sector has moved forward in large part by fully embracing the precepts of safety. To that end, after the headlines and spotlights of the X-Prize success came more science, more engineering, more self-examination and a preference for caution and methodical process. "Test and develop, test and develop, and do not fly until you are ready to fly" became the order of the day.

The time was well spent. As circumstances have changed and budgets have tightened, NASA has returned to its core mission of research and development, and technology demonstration. NASA is looking now to the Commercial Spaceflight industry for vital services. And the industry is delivering.

For years—for challenging years—the commercial space industry has contended with skepticism. Now it must deal with the effects of enthusiasm. Both of those can be equally daunting. Skeptics used to say the industry couldn't do it. Now there's the risk of new enthusiasts saying "do it this way, do it that way, or the industry needs to change its aim" just as commercial space reaches its target.

That's why I believe this is a key moment for special discernment when we must see clearly how commercial space flight got to where it is and how those responsible for it need to proceed and be supported.

The Office of Commercial Space Transportation (AST)

Congress took a major leap of faith with passage of the Commercial Space Act of 1984, legislating a framework when, practically speaking, there was so little real data on which to base choices. Fortunately, Congress produced a flexible, open venue that invited opportunity rather than proscribing innovation. This open venue will yield unparalleled benefits in due time and it all began with an Act of Congress.

A visionary product of the 1984 legislation was the Office of Commercial Space Transportation (AST). It began life in the Office of the Secretary of Transportation. It migrated successfully to a new status as one of the FAA's major lines of business. It was a fortunate turn of events. It enabled the early AST leadership to observe and absorb established safety practices and to build on them as it has helped guide an industry from the nursery to emerging maturity.

The industry and the office continue to evolve. An increasing number of tests and accelerating data collection will provide a clearer picture of what future regulatory steps may be in order. Scientist and regulator alike will learn more as manifests for operational flights become more robust and trips to suborbital space become regularly scheduled flights. Commercial spaceports operating as national assets will connect other launch sites as part of a transport and national security resource. Commercial space transportation will take its rightful place as a respected, recognized and, indeed, required part of our national transport grid. We are in an enriching learning environment where the growth in information will help us do better what we have already done well.

AST has proven itself a balanced advocate but firm regulator. I am not suggesting that the way things are, is entirely comfortable or ideal for either the regulator or the entrepreneur. Yet healthy tension and constructive disagreement are valuable commodities in a risk-persistent environment like rocket flight. And all parties have managed well.

Neither entrepreneur nor regulator has a monopoly on knowing what's best in every case. So they have worked hard—together—to keep finding out what's best. And that's proven to be the genius of the commercial space flight regime Congress established. In fact, the legislative/regulatory model now in place has worked to the credit of the industry, to the credit of the regulators and to the envy of space efforts in countries around the world.

Therefore, on any list of policy proposals:

I would unreservedly favor keeping the Office of Commercial Space Transportation within the FAA, for the near term, while a more robust launch manifest emerges. Although the Commercial Space Launch Act was approved at a time when hard data was scarce, the Act allowed the industry to establish itself. In 1984, despite limited data, we had little choice. Now we do.

Since we are still moving toward regularly scheduled launches in private human spaceflight, I believe we should take advantage of the pending opportunity to allow performance data to guide our way and inform our judgment. The Office of Commercial Space Transportation (AST) located with the Federal Aviation Administration is, I believe, in the best position to gather essential data on which Congress can base future choices.

At the same time, I believe Congress may be the best place to resolve jurisdictional questions surrounding hybrid space vehicles, those vehicles that have both space and aviation—like elements. These vehicles are designed for placing payloads or humans on either suborbital or orbital trajectories. They are built by a few companies in low volumes. Vehicle type and production certification is prohibitive in terms of cost and performance. Congress could address the issue, and then assign responsibilities to a supervising regulatory agency, the FAA.

Sub-orbital Launch Operations

I would propose that AST continue to supervise and solely regulate sub-orbital commercial launch operations. That would extend to any and all activities associated with rocket launches of either humans or cargo. This is especially important for launch operators like Virgin Galactic and other similar air-launched systems. The FAA's Office of Commercial Space Transportation licenses the launch system as a whole, but the FAA's Office of Aviation Safety (AVS) certificates the carrier aircraft when the aircraft is flying alone—even when that aircraft is operating in support of launch-related activities. This inefficient "dual license" requirement should be reconsidered. Managing two regulatory regimes for nearly similar operations risks introducing inconsistencies and gaps between regulation which could affect safety.

A related issue is the automatic revocation of an experimental permit upon issuance of a license. This "permit invalidation" inhibits smooth, rapid improvements in safety and capability. The CSLA should allow experimental permits to be valid for a particular design of a reusable suborbital rocket after a launch license has been issued for launch or reentry of a rocket of that design. Failure to resolve this issue produces cost, time lost, and uncertainty. Resolving this issue is a specific step Congress can take to assist the industry's growth and development.

Strengthen "informed consent"

While the Commercial Space Launch Act requires the licensees obtain informed consent from their spaceflight participant customers, it is silent on the issue of potential claims from participants in the event of a flight incident or accident. I recommend that the statue should allow for agreements not to sue, to include participants. These would be agreements under which all parties agree not to sue each other for any harm they may suffer, known as reciprocal waivers of claim.

Launch Site Safety

Safety governs the future of space operations. It is at the core of both the work AST does, and the success of the commercial space flight industry. To that end, in September of 2007, the Air Force and the FAA entered into a Memorandum of Agreement on Safety for Space Transportation and Range Activities. It took years to work it out. But it has proven itself a useful, necessary and key instrument for enhancing safety on the ranges and understanding among the parties. It has made operations easier for new launch entrants at Federal launch sites. It has produced common standards for launch operations among the Federal and non-federal/commercial launch sites.

Memorandum of Understanding

Among other Memoranda of Agreement, there is also a Memorandum of Understanding among the National Transportation Safety Board, the Air Force and the Federal Aviation Administration regarding space launch accidents. Although fortunately there has been no occasion to call it into operation, it is, as I see it, the kind of guiding document that will make it possible for all the overseeing parties to work effectively together if the need arises. At this point, I believe no adjustments are in order.

Indemnification

On another subject, I strongly favor extending indemnification provisions for a minimum of ten years. The current one-year extension breeds uncertainty in the same way that a series of one-year contracts in the sports world undermines confidence that a long-term contract inspires. The indemnification provision is a recommendation that Congress is not obliged to follow. But it sends a powerful message that says to the rest of the world: "The United States supports our commercial space industry and is willing to share the risk." Indemnification provides our domestic commercial space industry much-needed leverage in competing for business with state-sponsored launch efforts in other countries. The absence of the risk-sharing approach—or lack of assurance about its future—would create doubt and instability in the launch industry.

Creative approaches to acquisition

Space Act Agreements (SAAs) are an important public-private firm-fixed price approach to space system development. NASA's use of Space Act Agreements (SAAs) demonstrates NASA's willingness to proactively engage the private sector to identify potential opportunities for commercial space companies to meet NASA's needs and requirements. They dramatically reduce NASA's exposure to risk and incentivize commercial providers to keep development costs as low as possible while maintaining the highest standards for safety. Space Act Agreements often are not funded—rather, they result in monies flowing to the USG from partners using (and paying for the use of) NASA facilities and services. SAAs allow the USG to write any requirements that may be desired into the agreement.

The work products are already demonstrating contributions to NASA's beyond LEO human exploration missions in ways that will reduce costs while enhancing capabilities. For example, Bigelow Aerospace's SAA will help commercial space achieve escape velocity from low-Earth Orbit. In fact, on next Thursday, May 23, NASA Associate Administrator Bill Gerstenmaier and Robert Bigelow will participate in a kick-off briefing on Capitol Hill to describe the SAA and answer any questions that Members or Hill staff may have.

Nationally Integrated Space Capabilities

There are now eight FAA-licensed launch sites in the United States, with others under discussion. I believe we should explore ways to facilitate NASA's use of these sites as a matter of economy, convenience and safety. NASA currently makes available services to orbital and suborbital companies and it seems reasonable to return the courtesy.

The integration of assets and capabilities also helps address the matter of what commercial launch sites are up to when they are not launching rockets, their intended core business. I believe it would be extremely worthwhile for Congress to require that the Federal Aviation Administration, NASA and the Air Force explore the value of involving privately operated commercial spaceports as part of a national network to meet overall American space flight needs.

On-Orbit Authority

I agree with the DOT/FAA Commercial Space Transportation Advisory Committee (COMSTAC) that on-orbit authority needs to be discussed. Currently, uncertainty surrounds jurisdiction and regulatory questions of on—orbit operations involving space transportation. A thorough look should address questions like: Specifically, what are the safety hazards and needs posed by spacecraft while operating in the National Airspace System (NAS)? How should the U.S. Government handle on-orbit authority? What is the need for on—orbit authority and does the FAA play a role in satisfying that need? FAA/AST should examine "space traffic coordination" and create scenarios and analysis exploring the issue. AST should simulate and model with the FAA's Next Generation Airspace effort how the integration of regularly scheduled space traffic would look in the NAS. FAA/AST should begin infrastructure studies to identify monitoring requirements for on-orbit activities to the extent required for space traffic coordination.

NASA's Educational Programs

Finally, I am very concerned about the cuts to NASA's educational program at a time when NASA is on a different trajectory and with a vision different from any before. Like every other sector of the space industry, commercial space is dependent on America's ability to produce and equip with a specific set of technical skills and capabilities the next generation of space professionals. It is vital work that needs to begin early in a student's educational journey. These skills and capabilities derive from the STEM disciplines that can support space operations today, and those that young minds can dream and create for the future. No one teaches what NASA does like NASA. I recommend that Congress take another look at the benefits of STEM education and reconsider the enormous investment value of NASA's education program.

Going Forward

The FAA's Office of Commercial Space Transportation has performed pioneering service in a comparatively new and still evolving industry. It has worked effectively with the Air Force and with NASA and with the industry itself. And while forging a regulatory framework, it has been an active, open and attentive companion to seasoned talent in its own environment. I'm talking about NASA. Its work in human exploration and crew and cargo transport is unparalleled. Those of us in the space industry understand that NASA remains a living legend, changing, improving, adapting to new science and exploration.

In fact, the United States' diverse spaceflight talent is a major asset that we are fortunate to maintain. Other nations have put objects into space. Other nations have put humans into space. Some have conducted commercial space launches. But no other nation has done all these things using the resources and genius of both the public treasury and private investment. With safety as its imperative, the United States has shown to the world the ability to integrate space initiatives.

No other nation has done that. No other nation has performed space flight as well as we have. And I'm proud to say, we're getting even better at it. We are stronger than ever. We have only just begun.

Thank you.

Senator NELSON. Thank you, Ms. Smith.
Captain?

STATEMENT OF CAPTAIN MICHAEL LOPEZ-ALEGRIA, USN (RET.), PRESIDENT, COMMERCIAL SPACEFLIGHT FEDERATION

Captain LOPEZ-ALEGRIA. Chairman Nelson and Ranking Member Cruz, good morning again. I want to say it's an honor to be seated at this table with my colleagues, and thanks for the opportunity to share some thoughts on partnerships to advance the business of space with you.

About a year ago, after 20 years and over 4,000 orbits of the Earth, I decided to leave what was arguably a pretty good job as a NASA astronaut to come here, and I did that because this is really important. I truly believe that commercial space flight is important to the future of our human exploration of space in this country. We're about to restore an imperative national capability, to democratize access to space, and to build an industry that I'm convinced will lead the world, and frankly, I can't think of a more honorable calling than to be part of it.

The Commercial Spaceflight Federation represents over 40 companies across the country that are working to make commercial spaceflight a reality. Their spheres of influence range from near space with science and technology payloads on high-tech and very high-altitude balloons, to suborbit, low-Earth orbit and beyond.

The era of commercial human spaceflight began with the fantastic achievements of the SpaceShipOne team that won the Ansari X Prize back in 2004 by sending a piloted, reusable vehicle to an altitude of over 100 kilometers twice in the span of 5 days.

In recent weeks, there have been even more exciting accomplishments that point to the beginning of commercial suborbital operations within the next year. One was a testing by XCOR of a piston pump-powered rocket motor. This technology represents a giant leap in the quest for a propulsion system whose reusability approaches that of a commercial jet.

And another milestone that was mentioned before is a test flight by Scaled Composites of SpaceShipTwo, a larger version of its predecessor, for Virgin Galactic. Its rocket motor, developed by the Sierra Nevada Corporation, was ignited for the first time in flight after being released from its mother ship at almost 50,000 feet altitude.

But as impressive as these vehicles are, there is a big difference between suborbital vehicles and orbital vehicles. In space, getting there is all about speed, and to get to 100 kilometers altitude, you need to go about Mach 3. To get to orbit, you need to go about

Mach 25, and you can appreciate that there is a pretty big difference there, and that's the reason that until recently orbit has been the domain of nation-states and their agencies.

However, in addition to ULA—United Launch Alliance's—incredible record of successful launches recently, Space Exploration Technologies and Orbital Science Corporation, in the context of NASA's COTS program, have demonstrated the ability to achieve orbital space flight. And, in fact, SpaceX has now twice delivered cargo and returned it under NASA's CRS contract from the International Space Station.

This space station represents not only an investment of tens of billions of dollars but is also an unparalleled research facility where scientists and other researchers from around the world can conduct experiments in an environment that is not duplicable anywhere, on or off the planet. We strongly encourage the Congress to extend the utilization of ISS to its design life limit of 2028.

I went to the ISS for the third time back in 2006, but unlike the first two times, I wasn't on the Space Shuttle. I, in fact, rode a Soviet-designed rocket and capsule called Soyuz. Since the retirement of the Shuttle, it's been the only mode of transport available to U.S. astronauts. But building on the success of the commercial cargo programs, NASA is engaged in development of commercial crew system that has already created thousands of high-tech jobs across America.

At the same time, using innovative Space Act agreement transaction authorities, it has achieved progress far in excess of that likely to have been accomplished in a traditional development contract, yet while saving the taxpayer considerable money.

But funding levels below those proposed by NASA have resulted in a delay in operational capability and, as we know, every year that we can't launch American astronauts into space on American rockets is another year of sending over $450 million to Russia. It's imperative that we execute this program vigorously, which implies, among other things, full funding or funding at the highest possible levels.

History is littered with examples of empires that failed to adapt to changing times and were thus dethroned by others who did. Our world is very different from the heyday of NASA budgets that commanded 4.5 percent of Federal spending. But by intelligently partnering with the private sector, our space agency and, indeed, our Nation can continue to lead the world in mankind's greatest endeavor.

I look forward to discussing with you some of the policy details that are addressed in my written testimony, and I hope that my comments today will help materially contribute to your formulation and ultimate passage of legislation. Thank you.

[The prepared statement of Captain Lopez-Alegria follows:]

PREPARED STATEMENT OF CAPTAIN MICHAEL LOPEZ-ALEGRIA, USN (RET.), PRESIDENT, COMMERCIAL SPACEFLIGHT FEDERATION

Chairman Nelson, Ranking Member Cruz, and Members of the Subcommittee, thank you for holding this hearing and for the opportunity to testify as President of the Commercial Spaceflight Federation.

The Federal Government has worked with the American space industry in innumerable capacities since the dawn of the space program. Companies like Boeing,

Aerojet and the David Clark Company have worked with the Department of Defense (DOD), NASA and NASA's predecessor NACA since the 1940s to develop many of the spaceflight systems that took our astronauts to orbit and then to the Moon. In the 1980s, the first wave of space privatization occurred, giving birth to a number of new companies and a fast-growing commercial satellite industry that reached almost $180 billion in revenue by 2011. The Commercial Space Transportation office, now at the Federal Aviation Administration, was also established in the 1980s, to regulate and promote the commercial space launch industry. Many of the advancements that followed privatization have been in turn deployed for government purposes, proving the value of enlisting industry as an active partner in government space endeavors.

In the last few years, the industry has undergone significant growth in revenue, employees and capability. Much of its success has been based on the tremendous support that NASA has provided in developing and providing technologies, supporting development of space systems and buying services from commercial providers. This partnership between the private sector and NASA has helped create an industry that can provide services to both NASA and private customers, while creating jobs all over America.

Under the old paradigm for public-private partnership, NASA engineers would design space systems and then offer portions under cost-plus contracts for competitive bidding. This has been a successful method for building one-of-a-kind systems at the cutting edge of technology that can accomplish missions never before attempted. However, as our presence in space has expanded, it has become clear that there are wide variety of necessary systems and services that do not fit that template.

The new paradigm, which has emerged to complement but not replace the old, has been referred to as commercial procurement. It changes the role of government, so that it is a customer and involved participant in developing space systems, but not the designer, builder, operator or sole customer. This approach has proven highly successful in reducing the cost of maintaining critical space infrastructure in the pioneering Commercial Orbital Transportation System (COTS) and Commercial Resupply Services (CRS) programs, while promoting the development of systems that can also be used for commercial purposes. The model is a refinement of one that NASA and the DOD used in the 1990s to develop launch vehicles still in use today.

Meanwhile, completely commercial space activities are thriving as well. American orbital launch providers have become more competitive on the world market, bringing high-tech jobs back to America. Suborbital providers are building and testing vehicles that will tap a worldwide market for space tourism and fulfill scientists' need for more frequent and inexpensive access to space. Other companies are developing technologies to mine asteroids for valuable resources, visit the Moon, and disaggregate large satellites into small satellite constellations.

Orbital

A year ago, SpaceX launched its first mission to the International Space Station (ISS). Coming less than a year after the retirement of the Space Shuttle, the launch captured the imagination of the American people, strengthened the ISS program, and ushered in a new era of spaceflight cooperation. Of course, one competitor is not enough for a competitive marketplace, and just last month, Orbital Sciences Corporation completed a test flight that took the company one step closer to ISS. These companies are replacing some of the capabilities lost with the retirement of the Space Shuttle and ensuring that the investment and jobs involved in resupplying the ISS are staying in America.

Unlike most other government programs, which tend to increase in cost over time, NASA's Commercial Cargo Program (CCP) has the potential for cost reductions. The vehicles and rockets providing cargo services can also be available for commercial satellite launches, NASA crew launches and other commercial markets. In this way the fixed costs of development and manufacturing infrastructure will be spread over multiple customers, lowering the cost of the flights for NASA.

Meanwhile, NASA has been working with the companies competing to fly astronauts to the ISS. The Boeing Corporation recently performed force and moment wind tunnel testing of an integrated test article including both the CST–100 capsule and the launch vehicle adapter. Sierra Nevada Corporation has recently completed its integrated system safety analysis review, demonstrating the safety and reliability plans for the major components of its Dream Chaser crew transportation system. SpaceX conducted its Ground and Ascent Preliminary Design Review and continues to do qualification testing of its Falcon 9 "version 1.1" launch vehicle.

Other companies are also working with NASA to develop orbital launch systems, including Blue Origin, who, under the Commercial Crew Development program, performed a successful pad abort test and tested components of a new 100,000-pound

American rocket engine at NASA's Stennis Space Center. That engine is now undergoing evaluation at Blue Origin's West Texas facility.

Suborbital

While many companies are developing and flying orbital launch vehicles, we have seen a steady stream of progress in the suborbital arena, where reusable vehicles offer the possibility of high flight volume. Companies such as Armadillo Aerospace, Blue Origin, Masten Space Systems, Virgin Galactic and XCOR Aerospace are competing to offer flights for private individuals, researchers and experimental equipment to altitudes above 100 kilometers.

Virgin Galactic has performed many glide tests over the last year, and in April accomplished the first powered flight of its SpaceShipTwo vehicle, breaking the sound barrier and kicking off a busy year of flight-testing. XCOR is building a liquid rocket-powered vehicle that will be capable of aircraft-like operations. In March, the company performed a 67 second test firing of an engine mated to the vehicle fuselage, the first firing of a fully piston-pump-powered rocket engine. Also in March, Masten Space Systems completed the latest in a series of unmanned vertical-takeoff vertical-landing flights for Draper Labs to test autonomous control systems for use on vehicles that will land on the Moon or Mars. Finally, late last year, Armadillo Aerospace conducted a series of flights, including the first FAA-licensed flight from Spaceport America in New Mexico by an unmanned liquid propellant sounding rocket with a steerable parachute recovery system.

Each month brings new accomplishments among a set of companies competing for a robust market for research, space tourism and other applications. A recent study by analysts at the Tauri Group showed a demand for hundreds of suborbital flights a year for a broad array of purposes. In fact, because of the operational benefits of reusable vehicles, suborbital reusable capabilities could be a disruptive technology that creates entirely new markets. The personal computer, although less powerful than a room-sized mainframe, was infinitely more useful simply because of its easier operation and came to dominate the market not by replacing supercomputers, but rather by demonstrating the market was much larger than anyone had anticipated.

The development of reusable suborbital vehicles is a truly American phenomenon, and one that is creating high-tech jobs in Florida, Texas, California, New Mexico, Colorado, Washington and many other states across the country. Many states and local communities are modifying existing airports to accommodate horizontal and vertical launch suborbital vehicles or building new spaceports to bring home the benefits of the suborbital revolution.

NASA has been admirably forward-looking in creating the Flight Opportunities Program to purchase commercial reusable suborbital flights for technology demonstration and development and for other purposes. By being an anchor customer for services, the program provides significant incentives for private investment while only paying for services rendered. The program issues calls for proposals to fly technology payloads and has seen impressive interest from the research and technology development communities, indicating a pent-up demand for inexpensive, regular access to the space environment.

Other Commercial Space Activities

Over the last few years, as the suborbital and orbital arenas have become competitive industries in search of near-term markets, new businesses have arisen to support and take advantage of new developments and push the envelope of space economic activity farther. A web of suppliers and service providers, some traditional aerospace firms and some from other sectors that have only recently become involved in space activities, support each of the companies developing orbital or suborbital vehicles.

Many states have developed or are developing commercial spaceports, including New Mexico, Florida, Texas, Oklahoma, Virginia, Alaska, Colorado and California. Testing and training facilities are providing venues to test equipment and train crew and spaceflight participants in the types of environments they will experience. Companies around the country are supplying spacecraft parts and subsystems, ranging from screws and fasteners to environmental control systems, engines and spacesuits.

Meanwhile, new companies have arisen that are pursuing business plans using new ways to access space to build novel businesses. Several companies are building and launching small communications and remote sensing satellites that promise to make existing and new satellite applications more available and more robust. Other companies are building platforms that can host scientists and individuals in orbit. Finally, commercial space has targeted asteroids and the Moon through the efforts of companies like Planetary Resources, Moon Express and Golden Spike. All in all, it is an exciting time for commercial space as early investments bear fruit and a second generation of companies builds on the accomplishments of the first.

NASA Programs

While purely commercial activities are a vital and rapidly growing part of the demand for launch services, NASA has expanded that demand to include delivery of cargo and crew to the ISS. The success of NASA's commercial cargo and crew programs has been encouraging. Unfortunately, use of the term "commercial" has become the subject of some disagreement. All programs have some commercial aspects; the companies that built vehicles in the Apollo and Space Shuttle programs were selling goods or services, and were therefore commercial enterprises. Rather than being "commercial" or not, all programs fall somewhere on a continuum of development and procurement practices. It is our view that those that display the following characteristics are closer to the "commercial" end of the spectrum:

Full and open competition. Fair and open competition is a fundamental principle that has driven the economic engines of the free world that now dominate the global economy. This concept is eminently applicable to the acquisition of space systems and services to limit cost, incentivize efficiency, and promote innovation. Too often in the past, NASA programs have ended the competition with a prime contract award near the beginning of the program. Maintaining competition through all major procurements in a program is essential, and the DOD has thusly used competition in many of its major aircraft procurements. So far, NASA's commercial cargo and crew programs have used multi-stage competition to preserve the competition throughout the life of the program, while still providing enough business to the industry partners to justify their investment. It is clear from independent analyses that the COTS program saved money as compared to the traditional development cost of a single system, even though NASA's investment was split between two companies. In addition to desired cost containment effects, competition provides critical redundancy–both technical and programmatic–that allows the program to remain robust much later in the programmatic cycle than is afforded by an early down-select to one provider. In planning any program, we suggest that the Congress and NASA put a high premium on preserving competition.

Milestone-based fixed-price payments. The COTS program has shown how much NASA can accomplish when using its Other Transaction Authority to put in place milestone-based Space Act Agreements. In the absence of a firm-fixed-price contract or agreement, the objectives of the contractor and agency can be misaligned. Without performance incentives, the contractor has little motivation to create efficiencies and lower the project cost, and absent fixed-price milestones, the agency is free to add requirements or change its mind midway through the program, raising the price of the program for the taxpayer. While not all systems can be developed on fixed-price contracts or agreements, in general, the more freedom to change the price, the more expensive the product will be in the end. Selecting the right firm, fixed-price instrument is also critical to achieving cost effectiveness. Where NASA is actually acquiring goods or services, a Federal Acquisition Regulations (FAR) contract should likely be used. However, FAR contracts, even firm, fixed-price, limit flexibility and are subject to cost increases when the government directs changes. NASA has been very innovative in using funded Space Act Agreements in the crew and cargo programs to take advantage of their low overhead and flexibility to achieve cost effectiveness. Since NASA is only "buying" the certification of these transportation systems, using a FAR contract only for the certification data keep costs to a minimum while ensuring NASA oversight and verification of performance and safety.

Well-defined and well-communicated requirements and standards. Proper program design is required to keep any program on schedule and on budget. The Government Accountability Office (GAO) has analyzed failing programs and provided appropriate guidelines to many agencies to help them manage programs more effectively. Unfortunately, one of the most damaging forms of mismanagement–requirements creep–is still a problem. In one example discussed by the GAO, the addition of new requirements late in the development cycle helped double the cost of a GPS-related DOD program.

The degree to which a customer can be specific about its requirements, and that it can define those requirements sooner rather than later, is of great benefit to the cost effectiveness of a program. Defining program requirements, standards and milestones early is difficult, and some flexibility is always required as engineering developments may necessitate a modified or alternative requirement or standard. In its Commercial Crew Program, NASA is seeking to strike the right balance through an iterative process with industry partners in the first phase of the Certification Products Contracts. This process must continue apace to avoid costly, late changes to requirements. By facing these issues early, NASA is following the best practices outlined by the GAO and other experts. The processes pioneered by the commercial crew and cargo programs show great promise and should be practiced more widely at NASA.

Anticipation of other customers. The nation's recent economic difficulties mean NASA's budget has been smaller than the funding profile laid out in the NASA Authorization Act of 2010. Meanwhile, NASA's missions have stayed fixed or grown. In order for NASA to accomplish the remarkable things we all expect of it, the agency must be able to reduce the fixed costs associated with maintaining the Nation's current space capabilities. Unfortunately, some capabilities required for NASA's mission are unique, and for those NASA bears all the fixed costs of development and maintenance. Whenever possible, NASA should avoid this situation by developing and using services that also have other customers, allowing NASA to insist that commercial partners invest their own funds as well.

In the case of crew and cargo transportation to ISS, the capabilities developed by industry in partnership with NASA will also provide services to a diverse set of markets, including commercial satellite launch, space tourism, sovereign space exploration and utilization, future NASA missions and others.

By implementing lessons learned from past and ongoing commercial programs, NASA can ensure that its investment is used in the most efficient way possible. NASA's Commercial Crew Program is currently the most high-profile commercial space program in development. Its success is important to the commercial space industry, but even more important to our Nation. In difficult economic times, extending the period that American jobs are taken by Russian rocket companies is a mistake. The success of the Commercial Crew Program will mean that we are no longer dependent on Russian vehicles to transport our astronauts to the ISS. Meanwhile, it has already helped create thousands of jobs in the American space industry and will create many more as it comes to maturity.

The success of the program to date is due to the highly innovative teams at the competing companies, the skilled technical team at NASA and the commitment by NASA to commercial agreements and a minimum of unnecessary overhead. In the current phase of development, the Commercial Crew Integrated Capacity (CCiCap) program, NASA has undertaken an inventive two-pronged approach that reflects the two related, but different, goals of the program: Help industry create a competitive marketplace for crew delivery services to low-Earth orbit, and secure crew delivery services for NASA that satisfy its demanding requirements. Under this approach, the development of the systems is primarily performed under milestone-based Space Act Agreements that keep costs to a minimum while still providing NASA the insight needed to ensure the vehicles are safe for crew transport. Meanwhile, NASA is pursuing a parallel certification process under a traditional, fixed-price Federal Acquisition Regulation-based contract that will make certain that any other information NASA needs to ensure the safety of its astronauts is provided. In this way, the two transaction authorities are used for precisely the reasons they were created: Space Act Agreements to partner with industry to develop new capabilities that are relevant to both the government's needs and existing and emerging commercial markets, and FAR-based contracts to secure a service for NASA to use.

Despite seeking and receiving proposals—called optional milestones under CCiCap—from the participating companies that would allow them to proceed all the way to first crewed flight, NASA has indicated that it is planning to move the entire program to FAR-based contracts at the end of the current phase, just over a year from now. The transition away from the two-pronged approach may impose an increase in complexity and red tape on industry partners, which could result in growth in cost and schedule. Another approach would be to exercise the optional milestones under existing or revised Space Act Agreements while modifying the current FAR-based certification contracts. In this way, NASA maintains oversight, controls risk, verifies safety and will get the safe, reliable and cost-effective ISS crew transport it needs in a timely and affordable manner.

The ISS is the crown jewel of our human space enterprise. To quote Astronaut Chris Hadfield, who just returned from commanding ISS, "We are leaving Earth permanently. It is a huge historic step and we are trying to do it right and it takes time, it takes patience and it takes tenacity—and we're going to do it." ISS touches all aspects of why we go into space—exploration, science, inspiration and commerce. NASA will soon have astronauts flying on ISS for over a year, providing critical information about the long-term effects of weightlessness for astronauts going to Mars. Science experiments like the Alpha Magnetic Spectrometer are peering into the mysteries of dark matter. And, equally exciting, ISS is creating a marketplace of space users—whether it's small scale projects, like NanoRack's MixStix, a small test-tube experiment platform, or very large projects like Bigelow Aerospace's BEAM module, ISS is the proving ground for orbital space commerce. These activities will drive the demand for space access and perhaps new installations in Earth orbit. We strongly urge the Congress to extend utilization of the ISS to its design-life limit of 2028.

As NASA plans for exploration beyond earth orbit, we should also keep the lessons of the commercial programs in mind. Where NASA's purposes overlap with those of commercial entities, non-profits, other government agencies, and other governments, it should pursue approaches that take maximum advantage of those resources by engaging early and on multiple levels. NASA should include the private sector in planning exercises to ensure that overlapping purposes are recognized and pursued. As partners, NASA and industry can ensure a sustained American human presence beyond low-Earth orbit, and expand commercial, scientific and exploration opportunities throughout the Solar System.

The commercial spaceflight industry has competencies that can augment and complement NASA's for spaceflight beyond low-Earth orbit. For example, commercial spaceflight companies are working to identify, track, analyze, and eventually interact with near-Earth asteroids, complementing NASA's own efforts. Congress has an opportunity to leverage this innovative private-sector activity; the same skills and technology that enable asteroid mining, for example, enable defense from potentially hazardous asteroids and a NASA asteroid retrieval mission. The same technologies that allow Google Lunar X PRIZE companies to develop robotic spacecraft on the Moon will help NASA to accomplish its goals for lunar exploration. Congress should consider inexpensive ways to promote commercial activity in deep space, so that these companies and their investors can help accomplish national objectives and maintain U.S. leadership in a new industry. In the meantime, Congress should make it clear to the State Department that international negotiations about space resources must take U.S. private-sector activities into account.

Other companies like those that have been involved in NASA's commercial crew and cargo programs could modify their vehicles to provide cargo supply to a mission beyond low-Earth orbit. We urge NASA to adopt the highly successful COTS/CRS model, particularly the use of Space Act Agreements, wherever possible in the development of exploration capabilities that could have synergy with commercial activities, thereby reducing the cost and enhancing the safety of these systems. In other parts of NASA's mission, such as the dedicated or secondary launch of small satellites, commercial terms should also be the rule. We welcome further conversation on how the commercial space industry can enable NASA to reach farther and do more.

Federal Regulations

With the Commercial Space Launch Act of 1984, Congress established an office within the Department of Transportation to license and promote commercial launch activities. In the 1990s, the Office of Commercial Space Transportation was moved into the Federal Aviation Administration and was also given the authority to license reentry operations. From the beginning, the office's mandate was to ensure the safety of the uninvolved public (often called third parties), and since 1988 part of that task has been to ensure that an appropriate level of financial responsibility was established for licensed companies so that there would be funds available to pay any claims in the event of damage to the uninvolved public or the Federal Government.

Since it has been several years since the last full reauthorization of this agency, there are a number of course corrections that we feel are warranted to streamline the regulatory process and ensure the safe and beneficial development of the industry.

In 1988 Congress set up a "risk sharing regime" to deal with potential harm to uninvolved third parties. This regime requires that license applicants meet a stringent financial responsibility requirement by compelling them to purchase insurance or demonstrate sufficient financial resources to cover third-party damage claims up to the amount that could be caused by a 1-in-10 million probability launch accident. Importantly, the Federal Government is in fact protected from claims up to this Maximum Probable Loss (MPL) by the company's insurance or assets. In the extremely unlikely event of an accident that caused damage above the MPL, the Federal Government agreed to seek an expedited appropriation to cover damage above the insured amount.

In fact, because of the tiny chance of an accident costing more than the MPL, the risk-sharing regime is scored as having no significant cost by the Congressional Budget Office and has been renewed many times by Congress since 1988. According to our calculations, the regime has an actuarial cost of less than $10 per launch. The insurance policy that a launch company purchases to protect the public and the government typically costs many orders of magnitude more.

Last year, Congress only renewed the regime for one year at the end of the previous Congress, and it will expire again at the end of 2013. In view of the powerful protection that the risk-sharing regime provides to the Federal Government as well as industry, we strongly urge Congress to extend it indefinitely.

While the chance of damage to uninvolved people on the ground is small, spaceflight is an inherently dangerous business for those of us who fly. No one should board a launch vehicle believing that it is perfectly safe. In 2004, as commercial human spaceflight moved from the drawing board to the skies above Mojave, Congress passed a law declaring that customers of commercial human spaceflight launches were not passengers, but rather active "spaceflight participants." Along with this declaration came a requirement that any company launching a participant into space must fully inform them that the Federal Government does not certify spaceflight vehicles to be safe, of the risks of spaceflight in general, and of the specific safety record of their vehicle type. I am pleased to report that the Commercial Spaceflight Federation is currently developing an industry consensus standard practice for informing participants of these risks so that they are fully aware of the hazards.

Because of the risks of spaceflight, Congress understood that litigation could arise in the event of an accident, and because of the many different companies and individuals involved in any spaceflight, that litigation could be extended and complicated, imposing large costs on all parties involved. In order to avoid this situation, the Commercial Space Launch Act includes a requirement that the parties involved in a spaceflight (including customers) sign reciprocal waivers of claims with each other. All parties were included in this requirement except spaceflight participants, which raises the specter of protracted and complicated litigation. We therefore ask that Congress include spaceflight participants in the waiver of claims structure, knowing that the waivers do not excuse gross negligence or intentional action. We also ask that Congress clarify that Federal law controls any space launch activity, including the enforceability of waivers granted by spaceflight participants, and that these questions be under the sole jurisdiction of the Federal Courts, to avoid having conflicting law in different jurisdictions on matters that are fundamentally Federal in nature.

In the Commercial Space Launch Amendments Act of 2004 Congress recognized that human commercial spaceflight was a new and innovative business and that improvident regulation could easily stifle it. In that act, Congress established the principle that the Office of Commercial Space Transportation could continue to issue regulations to protect the uninvolved public without restriction, but should initially only issue regulations aimed at the safety of crew and spaceflight participants based on specific flight incidents that led or could have led to injury or death. This regime has provided regulatory stability, while enabling the industry to find inventive solutions to challenging technical problems. Though a sunset date was inserted in the 2004 bill, that date was extended in 2012 to the end of 2015. We ask that this extension be continued, as the general principle of flight-data-based regulation is important to allow the types of innovation that will improve safety in the long run.

Another correction would ensure that vehicles could continue to be tested after they are licensed, in appropriate circumstances. Current law forbids issuing an experimental permit for an individual reusable spacecraft after a launch license has been issued for a launch or reentry of a rocket of that design, meaning that further testing of the vehicle class could be limited. A technical fix would allow companies more flexibility to improve safety and increase performance. It would also enable flight-testing of new vehicles as they enter service, something required as the industry matures into operating fleets of vehicles.

Finally, air-launched or hybrid vehicles are currently regulated by two branches of the FAA depending on the particular activity taking place, a situation that the Commercial Space Launch Act tried very hard to prevent. FAA's Office of Commercial Space Transportation regulates an entire hybrid system on launch day, but FAA's Office of Aviation Safety regulates the launch platform and spaceship separately if other activities, such as repositioning and testing are pursued. Having two separate regulators thwarts congressional intent, adds to the cost and time burden of compliance, and creates the potential for regulatory gaps and conflicts that could potentially have a negative impact on safety. We are currently pursuing a solution within the FAA, but a legislative solution may be necessary.

Conclusion

It is said that some of the greatest companies in American history were formed during recessions. Adversity can sometimes bring the best out of government programs as well as people, breeding innovation that seeds the next great round of exploration. I hope that as you consider legislation later this year, you think of the commercial space industry as a resource that can help NASA achieve its ever-more-difficult missions and bring a new energy to the scientists, engineers, dreamers and policy-makers who see space as a vital component of our next economic boom. Please let me know of any way in which the Commercial Spaceflight Federation can help.

Senator NELSON. Thank you, Captain.
Dr. Collicott?

STATEMENT OF DR. STEVEN H. COLLICOTT, PROFESSOR, PURDUE UNIVERSITY SCHOOL OF AERONAUTICS AND ASTRONAUTICS

Mr. COLLICOTT. Thank you, Chairman Nelson and Ranking Member Cruz, and the Committee. I'm pleased to be here and to address this committee.

I'm going to speak on the role of the private suborbital space industry, on research and education. A little bit first, I'm a Professor in the School of Aeronautics and Astronautics at Purdue University in the College of Engineering. Purdue is the home of 23 astronauts. In my position, I have been teaching and researching topics in fluid dynamics for 23 years. My research explores the basic fluid physics for improving things like pulmonary health, fuel efficiency in transportation, communication satellite lifetime, jet engine cooling and lubrication, and similar. It's a nice job.

I am active in spaceflight research. In this sense, I am a member of the Suborbital Applications Researchers Group, working with Commercial Spaceflight Federation. We're a group of volunteer researchers to promote research uses in this new industry. I serve on the Scientific Advisory Board of CASIS, the Center for the Advancement of Science in Space. I am principal investigator of the Fluids Education Experiment, scheduled to be launched to Space Station in 2014.

I am building payloads to fly with suborbital companies: Armadillo and Blue Origin, Masten and XCOR and Virgin Galactic, plus a high-altitude balloon company, Near Space. I have worked through experiment design, payload integration, and launch operations even with some of these companies, and I've seen firsthand how this privately financed, uniquely American industry is poised to deliver remarkable new scientific research capabilities.

Researchers need to begin now to have experiments ready to exploit these new capabilities for science that can impact our lives here on Earth. Already, my student-built payloads have flown with an expensive German payload on Armadillo test flights.

Now, three minutes of high-quality micro-gravity test time is ideal for a number of physical sciences, and others, which to look up or down from these vehicles with telescopes and other instruments for unique observations. Various biological, life sciences and physiological researchers have well-justified plans for studies from the small-scale, like cellular signaling mechanisms, to the large, that is up to many dozens of human subjects.

Our own atmosphere is so poorly studied in the mesosphere and lower thermosphere that little is known. It's even difficult to find an expert in this part of the atmosphere. Yet this region, which is above all the balloon flights and below all the orbits, is where these new rockets will fly and coast on every mission, thus enabling many novel studies of this region, which is already felt to be important to carbon transport in our atmosphere.

All these and other fields of science can benefit from launching quickly, repeatedly, and affordably on the new vehicles.

Already, this industry is impacting education. I teach a zero-gravity flight experiment class at Purdue every semester, building experiments for launches with several of these companies, and also now a payload for a NASA Flight Opportunities Program launch. Thus universities are beginning to be involved, too.

For high schools, an automated student payload is easily affordable and would be just the next step in high school robotics. Thus, we can couple right into a phenomenal and popular hands-on, project-based, STEM education program that already exists nationwide in our high schools.

I see every semester how Purdue students are pulled into the experiment program, become inspired by the reality of science and engineering, and make early career decisions or choices to pursue excellence in STEM topics.

People, perhaps you, often ask me for one good reason why these new rockets will be important, just one good reason. Let's try this one: these rockets will provide new research capabilities of value to numerous fields of science, and this will produce advances not otherwise possible.

Why not a second good reason? These rockets will fly from numerous locations and on short notice, so transient and one-time events in astronomy, planetary science, Earth observation and atmospheric research can be captured.

I can continue. These rockets will fly a research payload for a small fraction of the cost of traditional rockets. They will fly a research payload to space more gently than traditional rockets, thus more sensitive instruments can be flown, and also cheaper off-the-shelf instruments can be used.

Some of these rockets will fly the researcher with the experiment, which is really very common in most experimental sciences.

These rockets will be reusable, thus driving down the cost.

These rockets are developed with private financing, so research agencies pay only for the flights they need.

The great accessibility of these rockets will enable a great number of spaceflight technologies to be tested and advanced inexpensively in space, accelerating NASA's exploration mission and strengthening the American companies that produce spaceflight systems for NASA.

These new rockets will enable a great mass of small robotic student experiments from all ages of students.

High school space experiments? You bet. That's exactly what we're talking about with these rockets.

Undergraduate and graduate students in engineering and sciences can design, build and perform original space experiments within a year, within a school year.

It's interesting to note that numerous science leaders today began their careers as graduate students in balloon and traditional sounding rocket experiments.

So that's 10 good reasons I see for using these vehicles. They're good science reasons, they're good education reasons, and I think they're good value-for-dollar reasons, too.

We should use traditional rockets when their capabilities are required, but most research and education, or much research and education will make tremendous gains on the new vehicles.

I urge you, Senators, to help us jump into using this emerging United States industry broadly for science and STEM education.

This does require some money, and it needs continuity and leadership. A multi-agency, multi-year program would be ideal.

Now is the time to begin to create the impacts we desire from this industry.

I thank you for your attention and will do my best to answer questions for you.

[The prepared statement of Mr. Collicott follows:]

PREPARED STATEMENT OF DR. STEVEN H. COLLICOTT, PROFESSOR, PURDUE UNIVERSITY SCHOOL OF AERONAUTICS AND ASTRONAUTICS

Introduction

Chairman Nelson, Ranking Member Cruz, and Members of the Subcommittee: Thank you for the opportunity to provide testimony to this subcommittee on the important role that commercial space, particularly commercial reusable suborbital vehicles, are beginning to play in my research, the research of my colleagues across the country in numerous fields, and the development of new technologies at NASA and elsewhere.

I believe that we are beginning an era of low-cost, routine space access that will offer incredible new opportunities for the research community. Reusable commercial suborbital vehicles will allow researchers to fly payloads often, conduct more experiments and collect more data, for the price of one traditional launch vehicle. Payloads will have a gentler ride to space, resulting in reduced payload development cost and the opportunity to fly experiments that were prohibitively difficult to fly before. With short lead times, there will be opportunities to launch coincident with terrestrial and astronomical phenomena, providing astronomers and earth scientists telescope observation prospects from the edge of space. Some of the platforms will also fly researchers alongside their payloads, an exciting new addition to space-based research that will provide flexibility that can only come from having an investigator in the loop, and reduce the need for expensive and error-prone automation. Like researchers on ocean-going vessels, in Antarctica, and on research aircraft, space-based researchers will be able to more effectively conduct their experiments when they fly with them to adapt to discovery and to acquire *in situ* data.

The availability of reusable suborbital vehicles with other existing platforms, like parabolic flights and the International Space Station (ISS), will allow researchers to benefit from a full suite of micro-gravity and space environments. I am tremendously excited about these upcoming opportunities for my own research. I have performed microgravity fluids experiments at drop towers, led my students on more than thirty parabolic aircraft experiments, and designed two of the six tests performed in the successful Capillary Flow Experiment onboard the International Space Station. I have also flown research on several test flights of new suborbital vehicles, serve as a member of the Suborbital Applications Researcher's Group, and am now a member of the Scientific Advisory Board for the Center for the Advancement of Science in Space (CASIS). The full ladder of microgravity platforms is important for a broad swath of researchers, as it allows us to test equipment, improve experimental design, and gather data at one rung before moving up to the next rung in microgravity duration and expense.

Industry Progress

The suborbital industry has reached many milestones recently, and I expect multiple providers will be flying participants and payloads within the next few years. In the last eight months alone:

Blue Origin successfully tested their suborbital crew capsule escape system, which in the event of a pad abort will rocket the crew away from the launch pad, demonstrating one of the key safety systems being developed for their vehicle.

Armadillo Aerospace launched two flight tests of their liquid-engine reusable sounding rocket, STIG–B, marking the first FAA licensed launch out of Spaceport America's vertical launch facility. Both of these flights carried payloads developed by my students at Purdue University.

XCOR Aerospace performed the first firing of a full piston-pump-powered rocket engine, which will allow their vehicle to fly inexpensively multiple times a day, with aircraft-like operations.

Masten Space Systems achieved a record altitude with Xombie, their precision vertical take-off, vertical landing vehicle. In March, Xombie reached an altitude of nearly 500 meters, testing guidance, navigation, and control systems that could be used on future missions to Mars or other destinations.

Virgin Galactic and Scaled Composites completed the 24th glide test of SpaceShipTwo and a week thereafter conducted the first powered flight test. After being released at an altitude of 47,000 ft by WhiteKnightTwo, SpaceShipTwo ignited its hybrid rocket motor to achieve an altitude of 55,000 ft and a velocity of Mach 1.2 before gliding to a landing at the Mojave Air & Space Port.

With this kind of progress by suborbital companies, the first wave of licensed flights carrying participants and payloads are expected to begin soon. In addition, research payload development takes several years, and to fully exploit the new capabilities that these vehicles will provide, we must put in place programs now to create a pipeline of science and research payloads. NASA has taken steps to begin to benefit from commercial, reusable suborbital vehicles, but there is still much more that can be done in and out of NASA to take full advantage of all the opportunities these vehicles create.

NASA Programs—Flight Opportunities, and Payload Development

In 2011, NASA created the Flight Opportunities Program (FOP) within its Space Technology Mission Directorate to use commercial suborbital rockets, balloons, and parabolic aircraft for technology development. By serving as an anchor customer for research flights to space, FOP is enabling companies to raise private investment, fostering the development of reusable suborbital vehicles, with the goal of creating routine, cost-effective and enduring space flight research platforms. The program only pays for flights flown, placing development expenses on the vehicle providers and their investors. Through FOP solicitations, researchers are able to fly technology payloads to space, raising the Technology Readiness Level (TRL) of technology needed by NASA, demonstrating an application in a relevant environment, or testing instruments and experiments in microgravity before they take a costly trip to orbit.

Earlier this year, Near Space Corporation, a company that provides high-altitude balloon systems, flew a payload for the New Mexico Institute of Mining and Technology (NMT) through the Flight Opportunities Program. NMT was testing a monitoring system to determine structural integrity for space vehicles, which is important for reusable spacecraft re-entering the atmosphere. NASA will be able to use tested technologies like these in future orbital and suborbital missions. Next month, Near Space is scheduled to fly the first upper-stratospheric low-gravity aircraft flights with their balloon-launched glider in a flight test program that I am involved in through NASA's FOP.

By flying payloads like these, FOP can rapidly refresh NASA's technology base and promote investment by the private sector by supporting the early adopters of new technology. We researchers who fly early will provide the proofs of concept that pave the way for those who fly later. However, currently the pool of researchers that can get NASA funding for reusable suborbital flights is limited, as FOP solicits only technology payloads. For researchers such as myself, and many of my colleagues creating science payloads, the solicitations through NASA to fund our payload development and fly on these vehicles are few and far between. I encourage the use of broader science-oriented solicitations for suborbital vehicles, so that NASA will reap the full benefits from both the science and technology areas, and to encourage early adopters from a broader range of disciplines. Additionally, along with drop towers and parabolic flights, these vehicles allow researchers to gather the data necessary at a lower rung before moving up the ladder to experiments on orbit. Gathering initial data on readily available platforms will allow more researchers to confidently send their experiments to an extended micro-gravity environment, reducing risk and increasing utilization of valuable on-orbit tools such as the International Space Station.

The Principal Investigator for the very successful German Capillary Channel Flow experiment in ISS tells me that drop tower experiments and traditional ESA sounding-rocket flights were critical steps for his team to be able to design the experiment to operate so well in orbit. My Purdue colleague who is Principal Investigator for the Critical Heat Flux Experiment being built for the ISS tells me that his parabolic aircraft flight research history in flow boiling is why he was able to conceive and design the experiment, propose it in a NASA competition, and win.

Furthermore, the new era of affordable and frequent access to space is accessible to any Federal agency with research, technology, or testing needs. Spaceflight research need not be a NASA-only endeavor when this uniquely American industry hits its stride.

Scientific Applications of Suborbital Flights

Though there are limited funding opportunities for suborbital scientists, exciting research is already in development. In many cases, payloads are funded by a patchwork of internal funds and small grants, so the current research is just skimming the surface of the pool of interested researchers. If more science payloads are funded, scientists will be able to dive deeper into their respective subjects, and produce results that are broadly applicable on Earth and in space.

I specialize in two-phase fluid dynamics research, and micro-gravity is a powerful tool for exploring Earth-bound applications and is obviously vital for spaceflight topics. My research involves the observation of fluid behavior free of gravity-induced effects such as sedimentation and buoyancy-induced convection. For example, in 2014 I will be launching to ISS the "Fluids Education Experiment" on the existence and stability of equilibrium capillary states. This research grows from computational research I did with researchers at a Centers for Disease Control laboratory a decade ago, where we investigated how minute water droplets can obstruct lung passages. Some of my other efforts seek to advance the ability of engineers to control and gauge the liquid rocket fuel in commercial communication satellites. A Purdue colleague's research into boiling and condensation processes, as used in refrigeration, is important to both expanding our spaceflight capabilities and to improving such systems on Earth.

Many other researchers with different areas of interest are excited to use suborbital capabilities as well:

Aeronomy and Mesospheric Science: Suborbital vehicles will be able to reach an area of the atmosphere that was only previously attainable through non-reusable and costly sounding rockets. This portion of the atmosphere, too high for balloons and too low for orbiting satellites, is sometimes called the "ignorosphere," and will now be accessible for *in-situ* high-altitude atmospheric research and to observe radiation from solar or astronomical sources that is blocked by the lower atmosphere.

Human Physiology: The three to five minutes of microgravity provided by suborbital vehicles, including transitions to and from high-g's, could provide new insight for some kinds of physiology research. In-situ monitoring may be available for numerous parameters such as heart rate, cardiac stroke volume, arterial blood pressure, oxygen saturation, regional blood volume, brain activity, eye movements, and spacecraft reference data. While enabling as much of the public as possible to have a chance to fly to space, this research may also produce insights on how to better research human conditions on the ground.

Fundamental Molecular Biology: One basic read-out of an organism's response to environmental stimulus is the changes in gene expression that the stimulus evokes. This response can be very rapid, and the signal transduction and initiation of gene expression can occur within minutes of perception. This type of response at the molecular level has been characterized in the stable, sustained microgravity environment of the space station and Space Shuttle, but the gene expression profiles associated with the transition from an environment with gravity to one without has yet to be examined. Thus, molecular biology experiments (which can be configured for rapid fixation by crew or citizen scientist) conducted on suborbital vehicles represents true, unexplored territory that can provide insight into the fundamental processes that underlie the initiation of novel stress responses.

Fundamental Physics of Particle Interactions: Suborbital flights offer sufficient time in microgravity to obtain physically important results on the interactions of regolith, dust and other small particles. The flexibility, re-flight possibility and cost of reusable suborbital flights will allow scientists to investigate the basic forces affecting a wide array of granular materials in a host of environments with applications to mining, pharmaceutical powders, food processing, and the ceramics-bricks-cement industries.

Pharmaceuticals: Through the study of protein structure and function in the human body, scientists can better develop drugs to interact with them, and create effective treatments. Typically longer term exposure to micro-gravity is ideal for protein crystal growth, but results have been obtained in sounding rockets with an exposure of just 30 seconds to micro-gravity. Mitsubishi Heavy Industries is planning to use XCOR's Lynx vehicle to perform drug discovery research on mice that have already gone through multiple parabolic flights.

Large Population Medical Research: The large population of spaceflight participants with varying medical histories offers new avenues for research. They will help scientists build a database to compare the response to spaceflight of people of varying levels of fitness, including smoking, alcohol use, stress & behavior, BMI, high cholesterol, low cholesterol, and physical inactivity. The effect of various medicines in microgravity can also be studied among the broad population and in specific subgroups.

With the research that can be conducted on these platforms comes an equally large potential for discoveries, products, and markets. For example, I have worked with my University to organize funding that will allow Indiana companies access to a suborbital flight for industrial research.

Of course, as with any scientific technique, much of the value of reusable suborbital flights may lie in areas that we do not anticipate. By opening up a new regime of research, we set the stage for discoveries that we cannot yet contemplate. Some scientists and policy-makers portray reusable suborbital vehicles as less useful because they offer flights that are shorter than orbital flights, more expensive than parabolic aircraft, and that reach lower altitudes than traditional expendable sounding rockets. These are similar to the objections many had to the first desktop computers, which were slower and less powerful than mainframes of that era. Yet, a new way of operation allowed our desktop computers to become vital to everyday life, even as they shrunk over time to become the mobile device you carry today. Similarly, judging reusable suborbital by the standards of the current orbital, sounding rocket and aircraft paradigm is beside the point.

These vehicles will create routine, cost-effective space access, an improvement over our current space transportation capabilities in a unique direction. Research, after all, is not a linear path from discovery to discovery, or about building an ideal high-precision experimental setup and measuring the results once. It is rather about exploring ideas, some likely to be fruitful and some improbable, and learning about and testing a wide array of phenomena. History teaches us of numerous accidental discoveries that led to great things. By accelerating the design, build, test, fly cycle that is at the center of space research, we allow researchers to explore far more intellectual space than they could otherwise approach.

STEM Opportunities

Reusable suborbital vehicles offer exciting new opportunities for Science, Technology, Engineering, and Mathematics (STEM) education and public outreach. The American space program has been an inspiration to the generations that are building these vehicles and conducting research. Suborbital reusable vehicles have the capability to do the same for a new generation, by allowing orders of magnitude more students access to space. These vehicles, and the research and technology that will be conducted on them, will inspire the next-generation of scientists and engineers and provide hands-on experience in the entire design-build-test process.

At Purdue University, I created and teach today a hands-on team-based project course for undergraduate students, *"Zero-Gravity Flight Experiments."* In this course, student-led teams design and propose an experiment to fly on a parabolic aircraft flight campaign, run by NASA. Students experience the entire process from proposal through building, testing, and flying, to data analysis and reporting. In the past few years, through a partnership with Armadillo Aerospace, I was able to expand the scope of this class to reusable suborbital vehicles, and more recently, the International Space Station. Student teams are now learning to design and build, and then work with suborbital vehicle providers to integrate their payload. With new suborbital vehicles arriving soon, I see endless possibilities for students to get the kind of hands-on experience highly valued by employers and academics.

Currently, space research is often limited by the dilatory cycle of launches—when one experiment finds a new phenomenon, the follow-up might take years to fly. The period from idea generation through grant application, experiment design, assembly and flight, can take more time than a graduate student spends in school. Because of this, many students only work on a small part of a larger project, a practice that does not lead smoothly to creating the next generation of principal investigators. Removing the wait to get on a space flight manifest allows students to conduct entire research projects and complete theses in space-based research within the time-frame of a degree. A surprisingly large number of the leaders in planetary science, astrophysics and other areas of NASA science, including the current Science Mission Directorate Associate Administrator John Grunsfeld, began their careers by leading small investigations on balloons and sounding rockets. Suborbital reusable flights offer a way to accelerate that process and give even more students the leadership experience that can be vital for further scientific success.

However, university research and education is just the beginning—a much younger generation will be able reap the benefits of these vehicles as well. From flying class-built payloads to flying teachers themselves, a new curriculum to inspire kids to pursue jobs in STEM fields can be built around flights that take place during a semester or a school year. In a study done by Change the Equation last year, the number of STEM job openings outnumbered unemployed people by almost two to one in certain STEM areas. Senior alums in the aerospace industry speak to me of their aging work force. Last weekend Purdue graduated 108 students with aerospace engineering Bachelor of Science degrees, and about 90 percent are already placed into jobs, graduate school, or military service. Our graduates are in demand. We all must utilize tools that can provide hands-on training and keep students interested in STEM topics and research if we are to keep our workforce competitive.

Conclusion

As I look around the country, I see a new and uniquely American industry, featuring many of my best former students, making progress toward routine flights of participants and payloads. The rocket science they are doing does not always perform on schedule, for it is both novel and challenging, but the trend is clear. New vehicles are entering the market as operational research platforms soon and this will mark a new chapter for U.S. innovation, science, and exploration.

I am honored to have had the opportunity to provide testimony for this hearing, and I look forward to answering any questions you have. The suborbital research community is excited about the possibilities reusable suborbital capabilities will bring to the table, and we believe that excitement will spread quickly to a broader community as we embark on this journey of discovery.

Senator NELSON. Thank you all.

Senator Cruz?

Senator CRUZ. Thank you, Mr. Chairman, and I thank each of the witnesses who testified today for your expertise and your illuminating comments.

I want to begin by talking about the U.S. share of commercial launch right now. In 2012, as I understand it, there was roughly $2.4 billion in commercial launch revenues, and only about $108 million of that was attributed to the United States, and I'd like to ask each of the members of the panel why you believe that's the case and what can be done to increase the U.S. share of that business.

Mr. HALE. Senator Cruz, I would offer for your consideration much of the difficulty in marketing U.S. launch systems abroad stems from the ITAR regulations which restrict the use of U.S. technology, for good reasons, to prevent missile technology from falling into the hands of foreign states that could use it for bad purposes. But what we have seen is that this caused other nations to develop their launch systems and, in fact, take away much of the business.

I had an opportunity to travel to India for NASA in my last year there, and we talked with the Indian space agency officials, and they thanked us very profusely for ITAR because that prodded them to build their own indigenous launch vehicles, and they use them to launch satellites today, and they are commercially available, and we see that around the world.

So I am not an expert on how to solve this regulatory problem, but I would offer for your consideration that that is a major factor in making U.S. satellite launches non-competitive worldwide.

Ms. SMITH. Yes, Senator Cruz. Financing continues to be a barrier, a difficulty for companies who intend to do space launch, launch rockets. It has been and continues to be a problem. I think what Mr. Hale just said with regard to ITAR is a big one, although we are seeing some improvements in the export control area. But other launching states have taken full advantage of that by advertising a place to do ITAR-free launches of satellites, which works to the disadvantage of the U.S.

This has much to do with why I so strongly recommended the continuation of indemnification. At a minimum of 10 years on a permanent basis would be excellent. I think that it is important for all of us to recognize that indemnification is the one thing that the U.S. industry has as it enters into negotiations for launch with other competing launching states, that it can say its government stands behind it in risk-sharing mode. It's not an automatic provision. It is a recommendation to Congress for an emergency appropriation above what is required by the company to purchase in terms of insurance, and it's a protection for the government.

So I think that it will be really, really important for us to give as full consideration as possible to that, and that indemnification continue as a way of fostering the opportunity to increase market share.

Captain LOPEZ-ALEGRIA. Senator Cruz, I don't really have much substantive to add to the argument, but the observation is that this is a global marketplace, and to the extent that you can compete, you're going to be better at market share. So the things that Mr. Hale and Ms. Smith have identified, which are ITAR regulation or ITAR reform and an extension of indemnification to provide a more level playing field for our providers vis-à-vis the foreign competitors, I think is key.

Mr. COLLICOTT. Thank you, Senator Cruz. I don't work in that end of the business. I shouldn't speak as an expert here. I do speak to a lot of people and work with this in industry, and I would say that that exposure leads me to give you more confidence in what the other people have said.

Senator CRUZ. Very good, and let me ask a follow-up question, in particular Mr. Hale and Ms. Smith, which is what do you all see as the most significant legal or regulatory obstacles to the continued expansion of commercial launch operations?

Mr. HALE. I would have to side with Ms. Smith that I think one of the greatest things that would be of benefit to this commercial enterprise is continued indemnification. The high cost of insurance and, frankly, the uncertainties in the American legal system are of great concern to investors, and as we look forward to private industry providing lower-cost launch systems that will be competitive in the world market, we must find a way to ensure that they are reasonably protected in these areas.

Ms. SMITH. Let me speak first to the question from the suborbital sector side. We have an oddity of sorts in the FAA in that we have a line of business that has statutory authority to license, regulate, and promote the U.S. commercial launch industry, responsible as a one-stop shop to do that licensing, regulating and promoting. We have hybrid launch vehicles, vehicles that have aviation elements as well as space elements.

And the question is, as often arises in a regulatory agency where you have differing industries, who has responsibility when it is operating as anything other than a launch vehicle? I think that that is an issue that only Congress can resolve legislatively by amending the Act to make it clear that the reasoning, the motivation behind allocating that responsibility to the Office of Commercial Space Transportation still holds. It is very important to those launch operators in that it causes increased cost when they have to travel between two regulatory authorities. It could also cause inconsistencies when it comes to safety.

This clarification is extremely important in order to further that industry and not delay its business plans and its launch plans as companies move forward to become a part of a full-fledged industry sector.

I think that to the extent that commercial space has evolved over time, it's a cyclical industry. It has had several fits and starts, but it has continued with the passion and the intent to move forward to become 1 day a full-fledged line of transportation, a form of transportation.

So I think to the extent that things like indemnification, things like resolving any regulatory tangles, continuing the opportunity through the flexibility that is allowed in the statute for these vehicle operators to test and develop, do more testing and development, collect sufficient data to move forward, is extremely important and one that I would encourage.

Senator CRUZ. Very good. Thank you, and thank you, Mr. Chairman.

Senator NELSON. Thank you, Senator Cruz.

I certainly agree with you all on indemnification. I had to get down on my knees and beg to finally get indemnification extended for just 1 year, and this is no way to run a railroad. Businesses can't plan on this. So we need a multi-year education—and I agree with you, Ms. Smith, that we need to have it much longer.

Now, on ITAR, basically we've got a political problem. You need to do business in an ideal world, as you all say, in the international arena, but those who would do ill to the ideals and the policies of this country, you've just got to be realists about it. So as we plan our commercial space ventures, that's the reality of the world.

I hope we can solve the insurance problem of indemnification with a multi-year extension, and do that in this upcoming NASA authorization bill. On saying that we are going to do business with somebody who is doing business with one of the political enemies of the United States is going to be a much harder task.

Captain, you are so right on in pointing out the huge difference between Mach 3 and Mach 25. But right now, as you pointed out, the space tourism market is with regard to Mach 3, to get up to suborbit, have a few minutes of weightlessness, and then come right back. What kind of revenues do you see being generated from this space tourism kind of experience over the next few years?

Captain LOPEZ-ALEGRIA. Thanks, Chairman, for the question. I should refer you to a study that was done by the Tauri group that was released last year, commissioned by the FAA and by Space Florida. I think it came out last summer. If memory serves, there were some very, I would say, conservative assumptions predicted that the market over the next decade would be about $600 million. But that was, again, a pretty suppressed view. They had a growth scenario where the revenue was much, much higher than that.

Now, that is for the entire suborbital industry, of which they determined that 80 percent or so was driven by tourism, about 10 percent by research, and the remaining 10 percent was divided into six different other, smaller markets.

Senator NELSON. And so right now the cost for a tourist to go in one of these up to the edge of space where they can see the curvature of the Earth, a couple of minutes of zero-G and then return, the cost is what? A few hundred thousand dollars per seat?

Captain LOPEZ-ALEGRIA. I think the lowest price that I have seen is a little less than $100,000, and the high end is around $200,000.

Senator NELSON. And so realistically over time, will that cost come down per seat?

Captain LOPEZ-ALEGRIA. Absolutely. I mean, I think the providers are counting on that, and this technology that I mentioned that XCOR demonstrated will make their vehicle be a lot like an airplane where you land it, the fuel is non-toxic, it is basically jet fuel. You put the hose on the airplane, you gas it up, and you go again. So they could fly several times a day, and clearly the more times you fly, the more you amortize your fixed costs, and the cost per seat will come down.

Senator NELSON. So then it is realistic to expect that it's going to get to the point where universities could buy a seat to send Dr. Collicott's students.

Captain LOPEZ-ALEGRIA. I would point out that, in fact, they already have. Universities and other research groups have purchased some seats, and I would expect that only to increase as the price comes down, as you say.

Senator NELSON. That's pretty exciting, isn't it, Dr. Collicott, that you might send your class to space, to the edge of space, go Mach 3, a couple of minutes of zero-G, and then come back?

Mr. COLLICOTT. Yes, it is, Chairman. It's no secret, Purdue has a downpayment on a spot on a Virgin Galactic science flight. I'm not going to fly. We are anticipating 200 pounds of automated payload to advance a high-tech Indiana industry. Certainly, when word got out, a large number of graduate students came to my office interested in the opportunity, and we even had good discussions with risk management at Purdue about the feasibility. It seemed to me that to them it was just a new technology to an old question. We need to go do research, we need to go do activities, whether it is research in Antarctica or wherever.

So to me it was really reassuring that it's not entirely new news, and I do look forward to the day when a potential Ph.D. student walks into my office and says, well, Professor, I flew in space for my Master's degree; what do you have to offer?

Senator NELSON. Well, maybe at that point we've got orbital hotels or laboratories that would enable a student to go into orbit by going Mach 25.

But tell me, Ms. Smith, do you think that the FAA and NASA working together can handle all the regulations of this exploding potential new business of space tourism?

Ms. SMITH. That's a good question, Senator, Mr. Chairman, and I would say that absolutely, yes, making the distinction that the FAA is a regulatory agency. NASA is not. But certainly, NASA's experience in human spaceflight is tremendous. I don't think that the amount of experience, the lessons learned, the varied experience that NASA has exists anyplace else the way that it does in NASA.

So the FAA right now, the Commercial Space Transportation Office, has had the majority of experience in dealing with commercial operators. That's its business and that's what it has been doing.

Partnering with NASA going forward to launch members of the public to suborbital space and ultimately to space one day, orbital space, I think it is a natural kind of partnership that exists and will link itself together very, very closely as we go forward to actually have operational flights that take people to and from suborbit. So, yes, I do think so.

Senator NELSON. By the way, one of you mentioned that the life of the International Space Station ought to be extended to its expected design life in the late 2020s, and I certainly agree. You remember when this thing started out, we had just gotten it put together, and it was going to cease to exist after 2016. We got that extended to 2020, and I'm hoping that as the Station starts to show its value, particularly with some of these promising new drugs that are being developed in their initial research stages, something that the average person on the street can identify with as to the value of what's happening on board the Space Station, I'm hoping that incentives like that will enable us, then, to go ahead in the authorization, to get it extended in its life.

I want to ask Dr. Collicott, getting back to suborbital space, to what degree has your suborbital research opportunities encouraged your students to pursue careers in aerospace?

Mr. COLLICOTT. Thank you, Chairman. Certainly, they choose to come to our Department of Aeronautics and Astronautics because that is already in their mind. So what I think I see is that just when they get involved in these long-term, team-based, multidisciplinary, hands-on original projects, I think they start to see how much good work they can do and their interactions with the companies, be it FAA or Spaceports or whomever, it really helps open their eyes to the industry, the reality of the industry they are heading into, and I think it gives them great encouragement that the great achievements in aerospace are within their reach, that they can be part of the teams that achieve these great things.

So I see it as a great strengthening of their perhaps childhood dream or their childhood hope to get into aerospace.

Senator NELSON. Do your students come to you thinking that the space program is over because of the mental image of the shutdown of the Space Shuttle?

Mr. COLLICOTT. I am very fortunate in my job at Purdue that many of our students, most of our students come in pretty well-informed and are aware that NASA is still in business, we still fly Americans in space, the Space Station is still operational. It's really more of the thoughts that you mentioned. I really see it more as I'm going around town or around the country talking to the general public.

Senator NELSON. Well, that is a fact, and what we are going to see is that as the Mars program starts to kick in, and we will start to see the first evidence of that next year as the Orion capsule is flight tested, then that awareness of the human space program will return. Then, of course, whenever we can get Americans flying on American vehicles up to the Space Station, combine that with what's happening on the surface of Mars right now, and I think you are going to begin to get a gradual re-recognition of America's role in space.

Senator Cruz?

Senator CRUZ. Thank you, Mr. Chairman.

I'd like to address a question primarily to Ms. Smith and Mr. Hale, but would welcome comments from any members of the panel.

As you know, the FAA is currently under a moratorium on issuing regulations regarding certain aspects of commercial spaceflight. What I would like to ask you is if you can elaborate on your views as to the importance of that moratorium and whether it should be extended, and in what regards.

Ms. SMITH. Since I was at the FAA when the 2004 Act was first passed, we had a very, very clear sense then, and I think now, that even while the moratorium was in place, if we had an unfortunate circumstance, if we observed something that was not safe, then we would be obligated to step up our oversight, to begin regulating, to recommend to Congress that we take a different approach if that were to happen.

In the interim, I think the reason for the moratorium was to allow the time for vehicle developers to test and develop, to continue to collect data, to try things to see if they work, all operating under the broad rubric of safety, which is the mantra in the commercial space launch industry.

I think that things have not materialized as quickly as perhaps Congress contemplated at the time, and we have yet to have those first flights, operational flights taking people to and from suborbital space that would allow the collection of data.

However, every one of the vehicle developers that are in this market are testing, collecting data all the time, testing and developing, and they continue to maintain a position that says that they will fly when they are ready to fly, not before. So I think to the extent that the moratorium would be extended, I would say 8 years beyond the first operational flight with humans on the vehicle.

Mr. HALE. Senator Cruz, I'm mindful of the fact that the FAA does, in fact, provide regulations for suborbital flight today, but they are regulations to protect the public. So the FAA has an extensive licensing process to ensure that these suborbital operators are protecting the non-involved public and property, and that is a very important aspect of their work.

The other aspect of this is that everyone recognizes that in these early days, that this is an experimental, high-risk situation, and the spaceflight participants, the space tourists if you will, that are going to participate in this need to be fully informed of the risks that are involved when they take on this high-risk endeavor.

People in America today can take on many high-risk endeavors, backcountry skiing, scuba diving in certain places. There are all kinds of high-risk endeavors that the Federal Government does not regulate but to which we try to make sure the participants are fully informed of the hazards, and that I think is the basis for the current moratorium that these participants coming from fields, not first necessarily in aerospace, can be informed of what it is they are really signing up for and have informed consent. That is a very important part of the so-called moratorium.

And the other part of it I think also is that the Federal Aviation Administration is struggling with exactly how to write regulations for this new industry, and some experience in watching how the industry performs would be very helpful to the FAA as they consider what regulations might be required. To go out and write regulations in advance of operations I think would be a very onerous thing to the industry and probably not efficient from the government standpoint.

Senator CRUZ. Thank you.

Now I would like to ask a question of Captain Lopez-Alegria, which is that many of the concerns that we hear about commercial space have to do with the prospects of actual markets that will be able to sustain private sector efforts over and above the provision of services to the government. Can you share your views regarding the potential commercial space markets outside of the U.S. Government?

Captain LOPEZ-ALEGRIA. Yes. May I just add on to what the——

Senator CRUZ. Absolutely, please.

Captain LOPEZ-ALEGRIA. First of all, I would agree with both Wayne and Patti about what they said. First of all, the FAA is certainly regulating third-party safety right now, and also the reason that this learning period was put into place was to allow industry to innovate so we wouldn't stifle things, cutoff solutions to technical problems before their time.

But just from a philosophical standpoint, while I think eight years is a good number, which is a number that they picked in 2004, I wonder whether this industry needs to have that learning period removed, ever. I know that sounds a little drastic, but let me just walk you through that.

So, as Wayne mentioned, scuba diving, bungee jumping, there are a lot of things that people do that most others would consider high risk, and I would be happy to see regulation in the commercial spaceflight industry when the commercial spaceflight industry looks like the commercial aviation industry. When it is that routine, when you can get on an airplane just like it's a taxi or any other mode of transportation, I think regulation is appropriate then. That, to me, seems a long way off.

So I would just put out there as a stake in the ground that this is something that, as long as people can operate under informed consent and be well-informed of those risks, that we ought to let that work in that sort of more free and enterprising environment.

So on the question of orbital markets——

Senator CRUZ. And can you elaborate for a bit more on the deleterious impact that you think it would have if the moratorium were to expire on a sooner timeframe?

Captain LOPEZ-ALEGRIA. I think there are two things. First, while the industry is still in development, the degree to which companies can choose to use a hybrid rocket motor or a liquid rocket motor or some other kind of rocket motor, they ought to be able to choose that and not have the FAA or anybody else say, "You need to use a liquid rocket motor because that's what NASA has been using on their vehicles," or something like that. So one is the reduction of the set of options available to solve technical problems.

And the second is that in the absence of regulation, people can exercise their own judgment to inform themselves of what the risks are, and I do want to mention that Mr. Hale is chairing our committee within the commercial spaceflight industry of developing standards, and one of the standards is to define exactly what that piece of paper should say that the customer spaceflight participant would have to read before he gets on the rocket and signs his informed consent.

But to the extent that we have industries that have commerce based on people that are willing to do those things as long as they're informed, and that the government protect people who are not second parties to that, then I think it is more in keeping with our philosophy of free and open markets.

Senator CRUZ. OK. And if you had some comments on the additional——

Captain LOPEZ-ALEGRIA. Right. So, back to the orbit. I wish I could point to a study like the Tauri Group study on the suborbital side, and I can't. I will just make the following observation. I flew in 2006 with a so-called spaceflight participant, a tourist that went up to the ISS on a Soyuz seat, and I flew home in 2007 with another one that had flown up in the meantime, and every single excess Soyuz seat has been sold, with unsatisfied demand.

So clearly, there is a market out there. Now, are there as many people that can pay that kind of price as can pay the suborbital price? Clearly not. But the idea is that once you start filling excess capacity with non-government, or at least non-U.S. Government so they can be sovereign government clients or they could be private research firms or they could be universities, or they could be just private citizens that could either take three of the seven seats that are on all of these commercial crew vehicles to the ISS, use the national lab facilities that are up there that are dedicated to private and academic research to come up with some "Aha" moment, decide that, hey, I'd like to be able to do this on a bigger scale, go contract with Bigelow, get an inflatable habitat, have your own transportation, that's how the market is going to start. I just can't say when.

Senator CRUZ. Very good. Thank you.

Thank you, Mr. Chairman.

Senator NELSON. Well, that was my question: When?

Captain LOPEZ-ALEGRIA. It's hard to—I think even the folks who did the suborbital market would say it's hard to predict markets that don't exist yet. But all I can say, like the famous movie quote, is I think the answer is build it and they will come.

Mr. HALE. Senator Nelson, if I could just add on to that, it is imperative that we provide low-cost—or have the capability to have low-cost transportation to low-Earth orbit. We see a plethora of business opportunities that are proposed and discussed in serious matters in space, and they are all currently coming up against this cost of transportation to low-Earth orbit. And if, in fact, we build this industry that provides much lower cost to low-Earth orbit, there are huge numbers of businesses out there that would like to take advantage of it.

I think it's very difficult to put that in an academic study and qualify that in the ways that the folks like to see these things footnoted. But just from the amount of literature and the number of people that are proposing businesses in space, there is a huge demand for transportation. The question is how low can we make the cost for reliable and safe transportation, and I think American private enterprise, that's their mission, is to develop low-cost capabilities that make money.

Senator NELSON. In your opening comments, you talked about how you could blend commercial space opportunities with NASA's plans for deep space exploration, and you stated you could get components and fuel and so forth up cheaper through the commercial space ventures, and that would supply, then, the NASA deep space ventures. Do you want to expand on that, or does anyone on the panel want to expand on that cooperation?

Mr. HALE. Thank you for that question, Senator Nelson. I think it's very important to consider this opportunity. In the first part of my statement of commercial space supporting the deep space exploration initiatives that NASA has in their future is with the International Space Station. I mean, there are many people today that are anxious to go on long duration deep space missions, and that is clearly the future of where NASA is going to go because the government's role truly is to push back the frontier where probably the return on investment is a longer term than the business spreadsheets like for it to be.

Those long duration missions require different kinds of technology than we have previously seen, but they're being tested and tried out today on the International Space Station. It doesn't sound very glamorous, but every time I read in the Space Station Report that the processor assembly has broken down and the crew has to go fix it, that's another step on the learning curve to building a good closed-loop environmental control system that you're going to need to go on a month-long mission to an asteroid or a three-year-long mission to Mars.

Those kinds of technologies, even though we try to test them on the ground, they really aren't proven until they've flown in space and you get to see what an actual operation in space does to those engineering systems. That's vitally important.

So keeping the International Space Station going as a test bed, supplying it with cargo and crews, vitally important, and that is exactly what the cargo resupply services contract is all about, that's exactly what the commercial crew program office is trying to provide.

Having said that, there are many ways to explore deep space. The current plan that NASA is developing with the space launch system and the multi-purpose crew vehicle, the Orion capsule, I think are aimed toward those deep space opportunities. But every mission study that I have seen to go to the moon, to Mars, requires a huge amount of logistics. If you want to go back to do anything other than flags and footprints, you need logistics. I think it was General Schwarzkopf that said that armchair generals study tactics, and real Generals study logistics.

Getting mass to low-Earth orbit is halfway to anywhere in the universe, and if we can supply equipment, fuel, even crews cheaply to low-Earth orbit, that has got to be a vital link in ensuring that whatever deep space capabilities we go from low-Earth orbit in pursuit of, we have the material that we need to make them successful. So low-cost transportation enables all of that. That's what we're all about in the commercial space enterprises.

Senator NELSON. I agree with you. Why do you think it's been so hard to change the mentality in our American space program to get to that point that eventually that's what will happen? The commercial program will collaborate, supplement, enhance the NASA deep space program. Why has it been so hard to get there?

Mr. HALE. People in my generation grew up with Apollo, Senator, and that has been our model for how space exploration should be done. And the situation and the world geopolitics in the 1960s, that was the only way to carry out such a model. That could work today, but it would require a huge expenditure of taxpayer money. I'm sure that given 4 or 5 percent of the Federal budget, NASA could completely do that job.

But knowing that the United States consensus on how much of their national treasure we are willing to devote to space exploration is about one-half of 1 percent of the Federal budget—that's the consensus; that's where it's been for more than two decades— we need to see how we can leverage that to do those great things, and it can't all be done by NASA. It's going to take commercial advocacy, commercial efforts.

You know, most of the immigrants that came to the United States did not come—some of them did for political or religious reasons, but most people came here to make money, for economic reasons. And having an economic reason to go into space will become a self-igniting source of future development and transportation. The United States Government buys airline tickets to fly people around. It does not operate their own airline, by and large, so on and so forth. That's the way space exploration, space travel needs to evolve as well.

Senator NELSON. Anybody else want to comment on that? The question is why has it been so hard for the American space program to change to accept the fact that the commercial space program can be complementary to deep space exploration?

Ms. SMITH. I think that for many, many years, since the Commercial Space Launch Act of 1984, space was seen by many people who were not as passionate as we all are, we space enthusiasts and committed people to the evolution of this industry, many people simply did not think that it would happen. They saw space as in the domain of the Government exclusively and did not understand the role of private enterprise in fostering the goals of space.

I think from that point, it often goes to where we sit is what we know. So NASA, as the vanguard of space for the country, the agency principally responsible for space exploration, continued to feel that, and enjoy a reputation as it does now, as the premiere agency for space. I can tell you that even though the FAA was solely responsible for commercial space transportation, any time a rocket launched, people associated it with NASA.

That has changed over time. That is changing every day. And I think that the kind of partnership that NASA has helped foster with the commercial industry through Space Act agreements, the CCIPT program, those things will continue to represent to the American public what is possible through commercial space transportation as the government helps enable that.

So I think that is a part of the reason. I think another part of the reason is that people just simply hadn't seen it. Something changed in the landscape in 2004 with the launch of SpaceShipOne. Standing there at the flight line, looking at people who had traveled there from all over the country and the world to see this historic flight, to witness it, to be a part of it, as many of them had when the first Shuttle launch took place, was an astounding thing to see, and people then saw that as a real possibility, that we can do this commercially, that we can contribute to the nation's space story in a viable way.

So I think as we go forward and as commercial space becomes more a reality, meeting NASA requirements in terms of crew and cargo to the ISS, spawning other destinations in space, inflatables like Bigelow Aerospace; I think that what some perceive as a "space gap," that reason for not moving as quickly as we could have will change.

Senator NELSON. Anybody else?

[No response.]

Senator NELSON. Well, of course, one of the questions that Senator Cruz and I have to deal with as we get ready for this NASA authorization bill is the continued amount of money that will go into the commercial crew program. And, of course, I think the atmosphere is getting better because of the successes that we've seen, the successes that we've seen with regard to the commercial rockets and the commercial cargo. But in the past, it sure has been difficult to get people to recognize what a lot of you all are talking about.

Any closing comments from any of you all?

[No response.]

Senator NELSON. Well, it's been most illuminating. Thank you.

The meeting is adjourned.

[Whereupon, at 11:23 a.m., the hearing was adjourned.]

APPENDIX

RESPONSE TO WRITTEN QUESTIONS SUBMITTED BY HON. BILL NELSON TO
N. WAYNE HALE, JR.

Question 1. Your written testimony implies that decreasing funding for spacecraft development ultimately results in less reliable and more expensive services in the future. Based on your experience with the Shuttle program, how might budget cuts in the Commercial Crew Program increase future costs?

Answer. A well run and effective development program starts with requirements and promptly develops a resource loaded schedule which can be optimized to ensure the design and development proceeds as efficiently as possible and which ensures the vehicle meets all requirements.

When annual budgets are lowered, frequently there is pressure to decrease the emphasis to meet all requirements resulting in a final design which is more or less deficient from the original intent.

More often, decreased annual budgets stretch out the design and development phase meaning that the workforce stays assigned to the project for a longer time than anticipated which drives up the overall cost. Along with the schedule delay, the work must be replanned and rephrased which can lead to inefficiencies, again increasing total program cost. And there is always the risk during a replanning process that significant items might be inadvertently dropped again ultimately leading to a design which lacks some of the features desired in the initial requirements.

In almost every case when annual budgets are decreased, there is increased pressure to eliminate engineering tests and analysis in the near term. Without those tests and analysis—or even if they are delayed—design solutions which ultimately are found to be unworkable are pursued in the interim, again resulting in overall waste and increasing program cost.

In extreme cases, reduction in annual budgets cause reductions in the safety workforce which means that less reliable or less safe design solutions come to fruition and cannot be re-engineered to meet higher reliability or safety goals. A principle example from the Space Shuttle development was the decision early on—partially due to the development budget cap—not to provide crew escape provisions. All efforts later in the program (*e.g.,* post-Challenger) provided mere band aide solutions because the basic design was not amenable to a comprehensive crew escape solution.

Continuing the Space Shuttle analogy, the budget development cap in the 1970s required the early design to be more costly per launch to stay within the cap. A more generous investment at the outset could easily have paid for itself in a vehicle which was less costly per launch: for example by providing for liquid fueled boosters—more costly to develop but less costly per launch than the solid rocket boosters which were selected.

Question 2. In your testimony, you mention having witnessed the negative effects of bureaucratic inefficiency and of shifting priorities on the Shuttle program. Based on this experience, what lessons learned should be applied in developing both government and private sector space transportation?

Answer. The Space Shuttle was developed as a government-led activity; in actuality government civil servants made all the critical decisions regarding design options, development testing, and operating procedures. While the NASA civil service human spaceflight workforce was very talented and highly motivated, it became increasingly bureaucratic over time. Even minor decision required multiple board presentations and could be tagged by technical authorities for further review. This greatly impacted program schedules.

Additionally, technical authorities increasingly became more conservative requiring extraordinary proof in many instances that commonly accepted practices in the aerospace industry were adequate. The technical authorities, at times, were only lightly motivated to actually operate the vehicles and were highly motivated to ensure that no untoward events occurred on their watch. There is always a balance of risk and reward when operating a highly complex, high performance vehicle, and in many cases the balance tilted strongly toward additional safeguards. Much of this was of little added value. While safety is always the primary consideration in any operation, addition of analysis and testing which did not add value to the process frequently caused delays and increased cost.

The Space Shuttle program was burdened with widely changing requirements; initially built to replace virtually all expendable U.S. launchers, flying secure payloads for the national security community, etc., it was restricted from commercial launches and also from most security payloads. Considerable expense to develop launch capability for polar flights from West Coast launch sites was wasted. The potential to recoup money from commercial launches was eliminated. It should also be noted that moving from Space Station Freedom construction in a low inclination orbit to the building of the ISS in a high inclination orbit caused significant redesign and rework of the shuttle elements to achieve that geopolitically motivated goal. All of these decisions were made for good reasons but the result was increased cost and inefficiency vs. the original design intent of the Space Shuttle.

Commercial crew transportation is being developed with the intent to be widely capable of various missions and the government needs to be very careful not to restrict those capabilities by onerous and restrictive requirements.

Question 3. In your estimation, what steps should NASA take to minimize any long-term increases in the cost per seat of private sector transportation to ISS?

Answer. The single most effective way to insure low cost transportation of government crews to the International Space Station is to allow for the development of a robust transportation industry to low-Earth orbit. If commercial crew transportation business is limited to merely supplying the International Space Station, the costs will be high and probably escalate over time. If the government, through the commercial crew program, provides the impetus for a vibrant new industry then costs will be low and probably decrease over time.

Developing a vibrant commercial crew transportation industry requires nuanced incentives from the government. Already the seed money for the program is allowing development of new vehicles. A light hand regarding early regulation is required for the developing industry to grow. Over burdening requirements can stifle development. Currently the NASA 1100 series of requirements for commercial crew is vastly more restrictive than what was envisioned at the start of the program. Those documents represent much of the old school of thinking in the NASA civil service workforce and have already suppressed innovative design solutions to some degree. Using the NASA requirements documents as a basis for FAA regulations, for example, would prove fatal to the fledgling industry and must be avoided.

Space transportation is a high risk activity and must be recognized for what it is. No amount of government restriction, requirement, or regulation will make it as safe as commercial air transportation in the near term and that fact must be recognized. Over time, with increased commercial success, increasing standards and gradual government regulation can improve safety; but the important element to improve safety and efficiency is to allow multiple commercial organizations to build multiple innovative vehicles to mature the state of practice in the engineering which will underlie the new industry.

Question 4. Given the technical differences between sub-orbital and orbital spaceflight, what policy differentiations should Congress consider when amending the Commercial Space Launch Act?

Answer. The suborbital market is nearer to commercial success in terms of space tourism and short duration microgravity research. The costs are much lower for suborbital spaceflight than for orbital spaceflight. Ultimately, orbital spaceflight has much higher potential for both tourism and research but the costs must be significantly lowered which will be a long-term proposition.

The energies involved and the hazard potential of orbital spaceflight are significantly greater than suborbital spaceflight. Protection of the public requires much greater attention for orbital vehicles than for suborbital ones.

Neither industry—commercial suborbital space or commercial orbital space—has yet had commercial success. At the current time, the light hand that is levied by the FAA on both types of commercial space access is appropriate and should be continued until the industries reach a level of commercial viability.

Given the relatively low cost of entry for suborbital spaceflight, it is still of great concern for the success of the industry that the government not act to increase those costs. When multiple vehicles are flying with commercial success, it may be appropriate to increase government oversight. At the current time, however, no increased scrutiny is necessary.

Orbital spaceflight due to the potential for more hazard, will require an increased level of government activity. However, given the already significant costs of orbital spaceflight, the government can achieve safety goals that only increase launch costs incrementally. Again, current levels of FAA regulation appear appropriate.

Question 5. In your estimation, should sub-orbital space flight be regulated as aviation or as a space endeavor? What technical and policy considerations lead to this conclusion?

Answer. Suborbital spaceflight is much more technically challenging than commercial aviation. Until a basis for the industry is established, additional regulation will be counter productive.

During the early years of aviation, when safety was low by today's standards, the greatest increase in safe practices and designs came from the development of multiple vehicles and their operation. Learning proceeded from practice. Government regulation followed.

Today's government safety regulations on commercial air travel are entirely justified for a mature industry. That same level of regulation cannot be appropriately developed for commercial suborbital space travel because the body of practice has not developed to an equivalent level. Establishing new government regulation for the suborbital spaceflight enterprise would be speculative based on aircraft practices which are not readily correlated. New regulations at this stage could be counterproductive to safety. New regulations at this stage would certainly inhibit the establishment of an industry.

In summary, the state of engineering practice for suborbital spaceflight is not mature enough to delineate new government regulations. It is only through the practice of developing new vehicles and testing them through operations that such practices will develop. After those practices develop, as they have in other mature industries, appropriate regulation becomes possible.

———

RESPONSE TO WRITTEN QUESTIONS SUBMITTED BY HON. BILL NELSON TO
PATTI GRACE SMITH

Question 1. Given the technical differences between sub-orbital and orbital spaceflight, what policy differentiations should Congress consider when amending the Commercial Space Launch Act?

Answer. Certainly no one would argue that the challenge is not greater when considering the operations of an orbital vehicle versus a suborbital one. If the vehicle is designed to carry humans, for certain additional safety requirements will need to be required. The Experimental Permit provision of the CSLA of 2004 is a great benchmark for the development of both suborbital and orbital vehicles that plan to carry humans to and from space.

For both suborbital and orbital flights, I would recommend cross-waivers among all parties be included in the license for the launch activity. Congress should clearly assert that only Federal courts may decide legal cases regarding an element of the Federal license, including the legal validity of any waiver of claims signed by a spaceflight participant, once the participant has acknowledged that he or she is aware of the risks and decides to go anyway.

Requirements for orbital flight are known throughout NASA's 100 series of documents and SSP 50808. SSP 50808 was established as the standard for any ISS mission. Further commercial crew development will be at Critical Design Review level by the time of phase II of the CCiCap program—and therefore key design requirements should already be known and understood. For NASA crew flights, a legislative clarification is necessary to ensure indemnification is applicable for these flights, whether through NASA Authorization or an FAA-issued license.

Question 2. In your estimation, should suborbital spaceflight be regulated as aviation or as a space endeavor? What technical and policy considerations lead to this conclusion?

Answer. Suborbital spaceflight should be regulated as a space endeavor. There is no one-to-one comparison between air and space, though similarities do exist. However, space flight is a unique enterprise.

As legislation has evolved over time, it has acknowledged the evolutionary nature of space. It has allowed for a regulatory approach that has recognized its uniqueness, rather than risk the tendency to over-regulate before it really gets off the ground. Clearly, this approach has given commercial space the opportunity it has needed without compromising the safety of the uninvolved public. It has never had to call upon its risk-sharing regime, indemnification, given that there have been no accidents that resulted in loss of life or significant property damage.

The beginning days of aviation saw many accidents as it developed into the mature industry it is today. Space is growing and evolving and will one day join the ranks of mature transportation. But until that time, Congress should continue to support the one-stop shop approach the industry has enjoyed with the passage of the CSLA of 1984. FAA/AST should be designated as that one stop within the FAA where commercial space launches and launch related activities begin and end. The FAA is well equipped with numerous other resources AST can collaborate with to arrive at the right solution. That end solution should be the sole responsibility of AST. To allow a "dual license" approach, *e.g.,* AST and AVS, places increased burdens on the limited resources of entrepreneurial companies and is likely to result in unintended consequences. Perhaps most importantly, managing to two regulatory regimes for nearly similar operation risks introduces inconsistencies and gaps between regulations which could impact safety.

Areas in need of specific CSLA language modifications:

- Recommend CSLA language be modified to specifically include spaceflight participants in third party indemnification.
- Recommend a legislative clarification to ensure indemnification is applicable to NASA crewed flights.
- Recommend Congress adopt the definition of "hybrid Launch vehicle" as a system designed for the purpose of placing payloads or humans on suborbital or orbital space trajectories. Vehicle type and production certification is prohibitive in terms of cost and vehicle performance, as these hybrid launch systems are designed to carry payloads into space.

Question 3. Currently, the FCC has limited authority to regulate on-orbit activities while the FAA does not, which means that companies must often work with multiple agencies to obtain the licenses they need to launch and test spacecraft. How might the Federal government bring these various functions together to ensure safe future operations while making it easier for companies to fly?

Answer. Currently, I am not aware of the absence of "on-orbit" authority being an impediment to commercial space flight. The DOT/FAA's Commercial Space Advisory Committee (COMSTAC) in responding to a question as to whether there was a need for on-orbit authority, stated the following: "A need for on-orbit authority was identified in order to facilitate space traffic coordination. No other justification was identified for such on-orbit authority by this group at this time". I concur with their finding and believe that it is an area that should continue to be studied and that COMSTAC is the appropriate entity to do so.

As far as the FCC is concerned, I believe that their statutory authority has to do with communications, not transportation. Transportation issues and regulations are best left to the DOT, and in this case, the FAA.

Question 4. The Commercial Space Launch Act tasks the Department of Transportation with both regulating and promoting commercial space transportation activity. The Federal Aviation Administration had similar direction for the aviation industry. Is this dual role appropriate for the FAA Office of Commercial Space Transportation?

Answer. Absolutely. The FAA/AST has done a superb job in keeping the two roles de-conflicted. While the office does an admirable job in promoting the commercial space industry, it does so without compromising its safety related, regulatory, responsibilities.

Question 5. How, if at all, would you suggest that Congress alter these responsibilities when considering new legislation?

Answer. I see no need to alter these responsibilities at this time.

RESPONSE TO WRITTEN QUESTIONS SUBMITTED BY HON. BILL NELSON TO CAPTAIN MICHAEL LOPEZ-ALEGRIA

Question 1. Your testimony states that the commercial industry's success has been based on "the tremendous support that NASA has provided in developing and providing technologies." Congress has supported NASA's Commercial Crew Program by increasing the budgetary commitment from $50 million in 2009 to over $500 million today. What are some specific achievements that have resulted from this collaboration? How would you characterize the economic impact of the private space transportation industry?

Answer. The Commercial Crew Program is now about halfway through its development stage, with three companies finalizing their design and building hardware for systems that can transport astronauts, NASA and private, to the International

Space Station and other destinations in low-Earth orbit. Each of the companies has passed vital milestones, including testing components and subsystems and passing design reviews. In parallel with these development efforts, NASA and its industry partner companies are certifying the vehicles to carry astronauts, a safety process that has never before been undertaken.

The commercial spaceflight industry has over $2 billion in private investment, and has created many thousands of high-tech jobs across the country. It has energized our nation's space enterprise and inspired the next generation of scientists, engineers, explorers and entrepreneurs. It is providing new, more affordable opportunities for scientific and industrial research, information technology innovation and new space-related goods and services yet to be imagined. I believe that commercial spaceflight will continue to grow in capability and beneficial economic impact, and secure America's place as the world leader in space.

Question 2. Given that any single private space transportation catastrophe would negatively affect the whole industry, establishing guidance for safety and mission assurance is critical. What are the major areas requiring standards development? By what process will the Commercial Spaceflight Federation seek to address them? What is the Commercial Spaceflight Federation's timeline for reaching consensus on voluntary safety standards for commercial human space flight?

Answer. The commercial spaceflight industry considers safety a critical priority, knowing that our customers, both private and government, expect and deserve the safest, most capable vehicles possible. We are committed as an industry to achieving ever-increasing levels of safety as we continue to innovate and grow.

Standards development is an important part of CSF's efforts to improve safety. We have created a formal process for approving standards and have five standards currently in various stages of that process. Our full membership will be voting on approval of our first official standard shortly. We are working not only with the FAA's Office of Commercial Space Transportation, but also the National Institute of Standards and Technology, as well as other established standards bodies, to ensure that our process is effective and appropriate.

The spaceflight environment is inherently dangerous, and different vehicle developers may attempt to deal with those dangers in different ways. Innovation in safety systems is also an important determinant of future safety. Therefore, we are beginning with areas in which standards can have broad applicability, including propellant handling, test notification procedures and landing gear. As the Committee is aware, we have actively consulted with the FAA on further high-priority topics for standards development, based on their data and experience. Going forward, we expect the typical standard to be developed over the course of three to six months and for standards to be updated as needed.

Many industries only develop standards once they have emerged fully and have a track record of operations on which to base them. Because our members' companies are in an inherently dangerous business and because of the public nature of much of what they do, we have begun our standards development process now, before the first flights for hire of manned commercial space vehicles, and expect to continue it in parallel as our industry evolves.

The reality is that due to the very nature of the business, and despite our commitment to safety, there will be accidents. Our goal, which I know is shared by the Committee, is to anticipate and avoid problems as well as we can, learn from our mistakes (small as well as large) that we do make, and continuously improve safety throughout the industry, for all of our customers—private and government.

Question 3. Given the technical differences between sub-orbital and orbital spaceflight, what policy differentiations should Congress consider when amending the Commercial Space Launch Act?

Answer. Although there are clearly some policy issues that impact suborbital and orbital spaceflight differently, we do not currently see a need to treat vehicles differently under the Commercial Space Launch Act.

Question 4. In your estimation, should sub-orbital space flight be regulated as aviation or as a space endeavor? What technical and policy considerations lead to this conclusion?

Answer. We believe that suborbital spaceflight should generally be regulated as spaceflight, because to do otherwise would a detriment to both aviation and spaceflight regulation. Suborbital spacecraft are different in character and function from commercial or private aircraft and will not initially be as safe as certified aircraft due to the maturity of the technologies, the flight environment in which they operate, and limited history of suborbital operations. The Commercial Space Launch Act appropriately classifies suborbital launches as space launches and the paying customers aboard as spaceflight participants, not passengers. To do otherwise would improperly burden an emerging industry with regulations designed for a mature one and could mislead the public as to the overall safety of spaceflight.

However, there are certain aspects of spaceflight in which the appropriate regulatory regime is very similar to aircraft. For example, suborbital spacecraft will need access to airspace, much like aircraft, and access to communications frequencies used by air traffic control to operate safely in the airspace. These issues are currently resolved effectively through local, regional and national authorities responsible for their use, including the Federal Communications Commission and appropriate portions of the FAA.

Question 5. In 1995, the Office of Commercial Space Transportation was transferred from the Secretary of Transportation to the FAA. Do you feel this is the proper location for this Office?

Answer. CSF does not currently have a position on this question. I would note for the record that this transfer was taken by administrative action and not an Act of Congress, and that the Secretary still retains the statutory authority and responsibility to regulate and promote our industry.

––––––––

RESPONSE TO WRITTEN QUESTIONS SUBMITTED BY HON. BILL NELSON TO DR. STEVEN H. COLLICOTT

Question 1. Drawing on your extensive experience working with NASA, how would you describe the role of the NASA Flight Opportunities Program in promoting the suborbital research market? Would you suggest any program changes to facilitate more research?

Answer. Thank you, Senator, for the question. There are two parts to this question, and I'll address these parts in order.

I see the NASA Flight Opportunities Program as having several roles in promoting the suborbital research market. In one sense, NASA FOP is aiding the growth of the industry by serving as a dependable initial customer of research flights. It is nice that they are not the only customer, and it is great that they are the dominant multi-year customer. This aids in bringing stability to the new privately-funded industry and to the marketplace, which benefits all researchers and American industry and jobs. Another role that NASA FOP is playing is that of making researchers aware of the research opportunities in this emerging U.S. industry. Through their Announcements of Flight Opportunities, broadcast effectively through NSPIRES and e-mails, the research community sees NASA FOP demonstrating leadership in research. Thus, I see that NASA FOP is advancing space flight technology and is aiding the sub-orbital industry in cost-effective ways.

To date, NASA FOP has concentrated on advancing space flight technology by buying flights, which is a great start. Researchers hope this initial program will rapidly grow into a broader mix of NASA-funded technology and science missions to address NASA's unique needs in both science and technology issues. Keep in mind that no other agency is going to spend their money to address NASA's needs.

The second part of the question opens up the topic of the continuation and future of FOP. I advocate for increased and broadened funding for the use of these vehicles by many programs within NASA. Why? Why should NASA spend money in this area? The answer is because this emerging industry provides a product that is ideal for advancing many scientific and technological programs important to NASA's mission and there is no other cost effective option. It's a simple business case; it's not scientists looking for a handout.

Programs throughout NASA can collaborate with FOP to advance science and technology and drive NASA towards mission successes. For example, expert researchers I talk to would see the following, in no certain order:

- Basic research experiments on granular mechanics in micro-g—asteroid surface-related microgravity geology. This will lead to understanding the geologic properties and processes of the surfaces of small near-Earth asteroids. This will support NASA's interests in robotic and human exploration of asteroids and the development of techniques and technologies for protecting Earth from the impact of hazardous near-Earth asteroids. Coordinating science funding for hardware and personnel with FOP flights will be a powerful step.
- Many aspects of capillary fluid dynamics affect life on Earth and space plus spaceflight technology. Partnering of the Space Life and Physical Sciences Research and Applications Division with Flight Opportunities Program would create a means to fund the research and the early-technology development required for success in future space exploration and with beneficial spin-offs to Earth-bound topics like micro-devices, fuel cells, and miniaturized medical in-

struments. Presently funding for such experiments is exceedingly limited and neither the research nor the experiment hardware is funded by FOP. Rapid development of experiments much cheaper than ISS experiments will be enabled by such collaborations and will benefit both NASA and life on Earth.

- As mentioned in earlier testimony, research into the Mesosphere and lower Thermosphere of our own atmosphere can benefit tremendously through the cost-effective use of these new vehicles. These flights will be frequent and will be higher than any balloon and lower than any satellite, and thus, the obvious choice for lofting many different instruments repeatedly into the mesosphere and lower thermosphere. Initial efforts should include: measurements of the chemistry of the mesopause region around 90km altitude to determine isotopic composition and changes in gases such as CO_2 and hydrogen compounds, studies of the energetics of the mesopause region, particularly radiative transfer involving CO_2, and investigations of winds and densities in the mesosphere and thermosphere using both in-situ and remote sensing methods. Experts at several NASA bases study various parts of the atmosphere, so it is not clear to me, an outsider, which people in NASA are best to lead this important effort.

- A basic read-out of an organism's response to its environment is the changes in gene expression that the stimulus evokes. This response can be very rapid, and the signal transduction and initiation of gene expression can occur within minutes of perception. This type of response at the molecular level has been characterized in the stable, sustained microgravity environment of the space station and Space Shuttle, but the gene expression profiles associated with the transition from an environment with gravity to one without has yet to be examined. Thus, molecular biology experiments conducted on suborbital vehicles represents true, unexplored territory that can provide insight into the fundamental processes that underlie the initiation of novel stress responses. The funding of fundamental science leads to the development of new insights and technologies that drives everything from pharmaceutical development to agricultural advancements. This application of suborbital vehicles enhances the success rate, and decreases the cost of deploying experiments to the ISS, and is a hugely valuable tool for enhanced science return in the space biology research community. It is also a valuable tool in the support of Florida's prominence in the spaceflight and space tourism industry. Kennedy Space Center is expanding their services to potentially include a suborbital provide and already caters to researchers and tourists who wish to use high performance aircraft to vet the hardware, science and people prior suborbital vehicle deployment

I also want to emphasize that not just NASA but also NSF, FAA, DoD, DoE, NIST, NOAA, DARPA, etc. should be looking now for how to exploit this new U.S. flight capability to uniquely and powerfully advance our Nation's science capabilities and their own programs. In the years ahead, NASA will be one customer of the new industry, not because it is in any way obligated to be a customer, but because the industry provides a product that NASA needs to address science and technology in a way to deliver on NASA's mission. The other agencies, plus other industries and educational entities, will also be customers for the same reason. This I see as the future of NASA involvement in the U.S. commercial sub-orbital industry. Is it best for this to be achieved through FOP, an evolved FOP, new programs, or standard purchasing methods as for other products and services NASA needs? That's not something I'm an expert in, so I can't say, but I will be pleased to work with NASA in any of these ways.

I thank you for the opportunity to answer this important question at length and I appreciate your interest in what a growing community of researchers see as an important part of NANSA's future.

○